# MUSHROOM CULTIVATION



N. Revathy
A. Vijayasamundeeswari
V.M. Indumathi
V. Gomathi

SHANLAX
#SINCE1990
SHANLAX PUBLICATIONS

**MUSHROOM CULTIVATION**



**First Edition: October 2020**

**ISBN: 978-93-90082-73-5**



***Publisher***

**SHANLAX** PUBLICATIONS
61, 66 T.P.K. Main Road
Vasantha Nagar
Madurai – 625003

*Ph: 0452-4208765,*
*Mobile: 7639303383*
*email:publisher@shanlaxpublications.com*
*web: www.shanlaxpublications.com*

# FOREWORD

Mushrooms have achieved significant importance due to their nutritive and medicinal values and as income generating venture in more than 100 countries. At present world mushroom production is estimated to be around 5 million tons / annum and increasing at the rate of 7 per cent/ annum.

The mushroom production technology can be profitably considered in areas where land is a limiting factor and agricultural residues are abundantly available. In addition mushroom cultivation provides some additional income in sustainable farming for small and marginal famers, landless labourers and especially for farm women. Large scale production of mushroom is also possible since there is a constant demand for mushroom especially in hotels and restaurants. This makes India suitable for the cultivation of different types of mushrooms. Besides it is estimated that about 355 million tons of crop residue is generated annually and about 170 million tons is left for burning and incorporating soil in manure form. If one per cent of this is used to produce mushrooms, India will become a major mushroom producing country in the world.

In India 85 per cent of the mushroom production is contributed by button mushroom *(Agaricus bisporus).* Oyster Mushroom *(Pleurotus spp.)* is popular in Southern states and milky mushroom (*Calocybe indica*) in Tamil Nadu. Oyster mushroom cultivation is being done in all districts of Tamil Nadu. Research Institutions and Stations of Tamil Nadu Agricultural University are conducting regular trainings and seminars on mushroom production. This book will be helpful to the students and mushroom growers for adopting good management practices for cultivation of mushrooms.

**Authors**

# PREFACE

In India, mushroom growing can be highly rewarding because of prevalence of malnutrition and the change towards vegetarian food among people. The mushroom technology can be profitably considered in areas where land is a limiting factor and agricultural residues are abundantly available. Mushroom cultivation is eco friendly. It recycles agricultural waste exerts less stress on land and water. And today mushrooms have achieved significant importance due to their nutritive value and medicinal properties as well as an income generation venture.

Keeping this in view, "Mushroom Cultivation" has been designed to acquaint students with mushroom cultivation and to appraise them with the importance of mushroom in their daily life and vital role they play in nutrition. This book covers a wide spectrum of chapters designed for students undertaking mushroom production courses in Agriculture, Horticulture and Home science.

This book has fourteen chapters and describes importance of mushroom, spawn production techniques, cultivation of mushrooms, pests and diseases of mushrooms, medicinal, nutritive value of mushroom and preservation of mushrooms. The content of this book have planned to cover all aspects of mushroom cultivation and it is hoped that this book will be helpful to students as well as mushroom growers.

**Authors**

# CONTENTS

# UNIT - 1
# INTRODUCTION

India is the second most populous country of the world with a population of over 120 crores. Increase in population is creating an alarming situation regarding food problem of India. Malnutrition in terms of 'protein' deficiency is one of the major factors responsible for high mortality and morbidity in this country and other developing countries of the world. Due to population explosion (100 million/year) the problem of protein hunger will become more and more acute. Exploiting non-traditional food resources can make a substantial break-through to meet the serious food deficit. Mushrooms, yeasts and algal foods are frequently mentioned as alternative sources of food. Of these, mushrooms are the most preferred. In the present circumstances, popularizing mushroom as part and parcel of everyday food is of paramount importance. Modern mushroom culture produces more protein per unit area of land than any other kind of agriculture and technology at present available.

## Food Value of Edible Mushrooms

The use of mushroom as food is probably as old as civilization itself. They have been a delicacy since ancient times. The Egyptians regarded them as a food for Pharaohs. The Greeks and Romans described them as *'food for the Gods'* and were served only on festive occasions. Reference to mushrooms is found in Vedas. These were earlier preferred for their flavour and taste, while their nutritive value was recognized later.

Mushrooms provide a rich addition to the diet in the form of proteins, carbohydrates, minerals and vitamins. The protein content of fresh mushrooms (3g/100 g) is about 3.7 percent. It is twice as high as that in most vegetables except green peas, brussels sprouts and pulses and is, much lower to meat, egg, fish and cheese. They have a high percentage of all the nine essential amino acids. They are low in calories (less than 35 K cal per 100 g) with traces of sugar and without cholesterol. These are richer in vitamins ($B_1$, $B_2$, Niacin, $B_{12}$, pantothenic acid and vitamin C) than most vegetables and almost free from fat (0.2g 100g). They are also a good source of minerals (P, K and Fe.). Thus they serve a valuable source of nutritive and protective food.

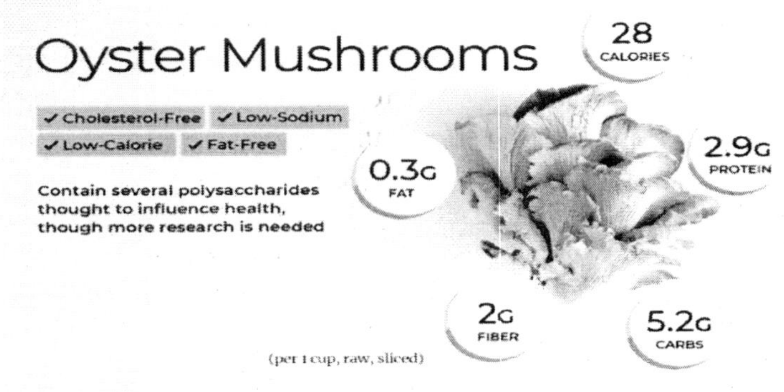


**Cultivated Edible Mushrooms**

Presently about a dozen fungi are cultivated in over 100 countries with a production of 3.7 million tonnes and the demand is increasing 15 % every year. Five genera, *Agaricus, Lentinus, Volvariella, Pleurotus* and *Flammulina* contributed about 91 per cent of total production. White button mushroom (*Agaricus brunnescens (bisporus)* has the largest share (56%) followed by shiitake mushroom *(Lentinus edodes) (*14%), paddy straw mushroom *(Volvariella volvacea)* (8%), Oyster mushroom (Pleurotus spp.) (7.7%) and others (13%).

India is blessed with its varied agro-climates from temperate, subtropical, or tropical. This makes India suitable for the cultivation of different types of mushrooms. Besides it is estimated that about 355 million tons of crop residue is generated annually and about 170 million is left out for burning and incorporating soil in manure form. If one percent of this is used to produce mushrooms, India will become a major mushroom producing country in the world. Though mushroom production started in 70s, it was during the 1990s that there was a sudden jump in its production, when about a dozen export oriented units were set up for the production of button mushroom, with the collaboration of foreign companies. This resulted in significant increase in mushroom production from 4000 tonnes (1985) to 30,000 tonnes (1995) and 40,000 tonnes (1997). At present it is estimated that production of mushroom in India to be 1,29,782 metric tonnes per annum (Sharma *et al.*, 2017).

Mushroom production does not require agricultural land and can be done on waste and unproductive land. Since it is done indoors, one can utilize vertical space for higher productivity: Agricultural/forest waste can be utilized to produce quality food through mushroom production. Besides, mushroom have high bioefficiency (upto 100%) i.e. conversion of dried wastes into fresh mushrooms. They help to recycle agricultural wastes. Spent mushroom substrate can be used as feed for animals and to produce organic manure or vermicompost. Mushroom farming is a labour intensive indoor activity which can help the landless, small and augment marginal farmers to raise their income, diversify economic activity and can create gainful employment especially for unemployed/under employed youths, weaker sections of the society and women folk. It produces nutritious food from unused resources, thus available surplus in India (355 milllion tonnes of agricultural wastes) can earn valuable foreign exchange.

# UNIT - 2
# HISTORY OF MUSHROOM CULTIVATION

**"Without leaves, without buds, without flowers, yet they form fruit: as a food, as a tonic and as a medicine, the entire creation is precious" - S.T. Chang**

The history of mushroom cultivation goes back to the ages of "VED*A*" wherein the mention was made in the classical religious scriptures like 'Rig Veda' and 'Atharvana Veda' about use of juice from fly agaric mushroom (*Amanita muscar*ia) as a intoxicating drink, named as "Soma". Mention was made about *Auricularia,* generally called as Ear mushroom or Jew's Mushroom as early as 300 BC in the Chinese literature, "LIKI" and in the book, "SIP' during 230 BC. In the early Christian era, the fly agaric mushroom was mentioned as "Sun of God". The Romans considered mushroom as "Foods of Gods" and served during important festive seasons. The Mexican Indians treated mushrooms as "Flesh of Gods" as the person who consumed *Amanita musacria* developed Psychotropic effect (Mushroom Madness). They also reported the same ill effect in consuming the species of *Boletus, Russula* and *Psilocybe.*

The Chinese considered Red mushroom *(Russula rubra*) as 'Elixer of Life'. Greeks used mushroom as medicine and they believed that mushrooms provided strength to the soldiers during war period. In 700 AD, a French Horticulturist cultivated *A. bisporus* in Paris. Tournefort, a Frenchman, was the first to publish work on "Mushroom Cultivation". In 1754, green house cultivation of mushroom was started in Sweden and England. Subsequently, it was cultivated in France and Holland in 1810. Green house cultivation of mushroom was started in 1890 in USA. In the same year Constantin first developed the mushroom spawn. However, Dugger did the first publication on spawn production technology in the year 1905. In the year 1917, cultivation of *P. ostreatus* was demonstrated in wood logs in Germany. Subsequently mushroom houses were built for cultivation This work lead to the spread of spawn production technology throughout the world.

**Button mushroom cultivation in caves during 17$^{th}$ century**

American scientist, Sindan developed the synthetic compost for growth of mushroom. He also patented the grain spawn process in 1938. In 1940, One French mycologist developed compost for *Agaricus* by mixing gypsum, horse manure and poultry manure. Later, Lambert of Wed States Department of Agriculture laid the foundation for modern mushroom technology. Subsequently, Sindan and others developed several synthetic composts for cultivation of *Agaricus.*

The work on mushroom in India started as early as 1918 when Kirtikar of Imperial Mycological Society recorded the occurrence of mushrooms from Calcutta. Later, Bose successfully cultivated two *Agaricus* on sterilized dung. In 1940, Su and Seth described the procedure for spawn and cultivation of *Volvariella*. However, the first successful cultivation techniques for paddy straw mushroom (*Volveriella volvacea)* was demonstrated by Thomas in the year 1943 in Agricultural College, Coimbatore. This lead to the spread of cultivation of this mushroom in all parts of India. But it is yet to be adopted on a commercial scale. Being a tropical mushroom, it is highly suitable for northern Plains as well as coastal and plateaus of South India. However, a very little research support has been extended of this mushroom in India because of its very low yield potential coupled with highly perishable nature of the fruiting bodies.

In 1941, Padwick indicated the possibilities of growing button mushroom in India. In the field of button mushroom (*Agaricus bisporus*), India, China and some other Asian countries, was late starters, making a humble beginning in the early sixties. In 1961, Indian Council of Agricultural Research, New Delhi, started first cultivation of *Agaricus bisporus* at Solan in Himachal Pradesh in collaboration with Government of Himachal Pradesh. Researchers conducted during 60s and 70s were more or less adaptive in nature and production technology developed lacked the refinement. Dutch scientists first developed the first hybrid strains of *A. bisporus* in 1981.

However, In India the introduction of exotic strains and testing their suitability for Indian conditions continued till late eighties as there lacks enough variability in the existing bispored strains of *Agaricus* due to high degree of inbreeding and practically no wild germplasm of *A. bisporus* is available in Indian Gene bank. However, due to the efforts taken by Indian scientists employing hybridization, mutation and genetic manipulation in the field of button mushroom, there has been almost an exponential growth both in production and productivity during last ten years, out put reaching 1,29,782 metric tonnes in 2016 from meager 1000 tonnes in 1985.

*Pleurotus* mushroom which is generally referred to as 'Oyster mushroom world over and as 'Dhingri' in India, has its origin from Greek word "pleuro" which means formed laterally or in a side way position, particularly referring to the lateral position of the stipe (stem) in relation to pileus (cap). Species of the genus *Pleurotus* are well appreciated for their broad adaptability under varied agro-climatic conditions.

The several species of this mushroom occur commonly as wood- decomposers in forests throughout the world. *Pleurotus* has always been most attractive to commercial mushroom growers because of the ease by which most species can be cultivated. In India, Bano and Srivastava demonstrated the successful cultivation of *P. ostreatus* in 1962.

**Cultivation of mushroom during 19th century**

After establishing the All India Coordinated Research Projects on Mushroom (AICRP Mushroom) at Solan, the research on this mushroom was intensified. The mushroom research projects have started running in various State Agricultural Universities, particularly in Punjab, Uttar Pradesh, Karnataka and Tamil Nadu. In Tamil Nadu Agricultural University, the research on oyster mushroom was started in 1974 and the first species introduced was *P. sajor- caju* (Grey oyster) and an improved strain of this species was released for commercial cultivation as M2. After implementation of All India Coordinated Mushroom Improvement Project at TNAU, Coimbatore work on mushroom research was intensified and a another oyster mushroom, *P. citrinopileatus* was released for commercialization and named as Co-1, which is commonly called as White Oyster. Later, *P. djamor,* named as MDU1 was developed from Agricultural College and Research Institute, Madurai campus of TNAU. The research efforts taken by the scientists of Regional Research Station, Aruppukottai of TNAU lead to the introduction of *P. eous*, named as APK1, which produces Pink fruiting bodies.

The continued efforts in TNAU, Coimbatore to identify and test the mushroom species with good bio efficiency led to release *P.florida* and *P.platypus* for commercialization. The research work conducted at Horticultural Research Station, Vijayanagaram, TNAU in the Nilgiris lead to introduce *P.ostreatus*, named as Ooty1 oyster mushroom and Ooty 1 button mushroom (AB1). A new milky mushroom (*Calocybe indica*) with high bio efficiency was released as APK2 from Regional Research Station, Aruppukottai. In addition to above mushroom species, evaluation works are being continued in some other mushrooms *viz.,* Shiitake mushroom *(Lentinus edodes*) and Jew's ear mushroom (*Auricularia auricula* and *A.polytricha*). In addition, regular survey programmes are going on to identify new edible mushroom species with high yield potential for commercialization in India.

# UNIT - 3
# BIOLOGY OF MUSHROOM

Mushrooms are the fleshy fungi, which constitute a major group of lower plant kingdom. The mushroom is a common fungal fruiting body that produces basidiospores at the tip of club like structures called basidia, which are arranged along the gills of the mushroom. Beneath the mushroom, in the soil is the mould colony itself, consisting of a mat of intertwined hyphae, sometimes several feet in diameter. The mushrooms first appear as white tiny balls consisting of short stem (stipe) and a cap (pileus), which begin to open up like an umbrella.

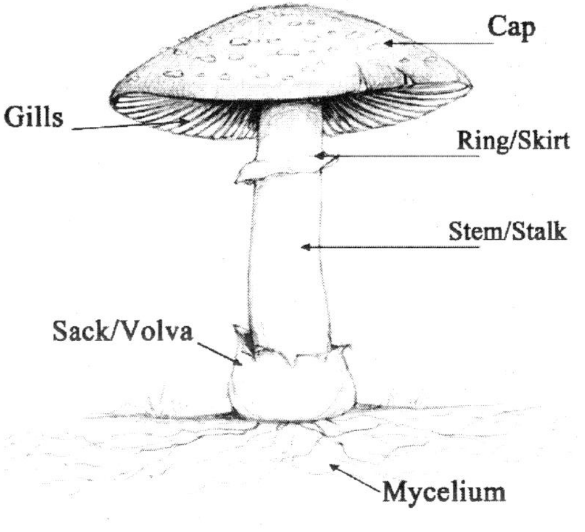


**Figure 1 Structure of mushroom**

The delicate membrane or veil (velum) enveloping the cap tears off, if allowed to develop fully, and lamellae (gills) radiating from the stalk into the cap become visible. These gills become darkened as the basidiospores develop into millions and fall to the ground for starting their life cycle once again for second generation of mushrooms (Fig.1).

## 1. White button/European mushroom/Button mushroom: *Agaricus bisporus*

Cultivation of *Agaricus bisporus* is a complex process and requires special technical skill for raising a successful crop. For its growth it requires two different temperatures, 25-28°C for spawn run or vegetative growth and 12-18°C for fruit body formation. Besides temperature it requires proper humidity during fructification (80-90% RH) and enough ventilation.

**Button mushroom**

**Taxonomy**

| | | |
|---|---|---|
| *Kingdom* | : | *Fungi* |
| *Phylum* | : | *Basidiomycota* |
| *Subphylum* | : | *Basidiomycotina* |
| *Class* | : | *Agaricomycetes* |
| *Subclass* | : | *Agaricomycetidae* |
| *Order* | : | *Agaricales* |
| *Family* | : | *Agaricaceae* |

## 2. Oyster mushroom: *Pleurotus* sp.

Oyster mushroom which is popularly known as "dhingri" in India. Oyster mushroom has three distinct parts- fleshy shell or spatula shaped cup(Pileus), a short or long central or lateral stalk called stipe and long ridges and furrows called gills on the under side of the cap. The gills stretch from the edge of the cap down to the stalk and bear the spores. Oyster mushroom comes in plains with temperature requirement of 25-28°C for spawn run and 25-30°C for cropping. All the species *of Pleurotus* require very high relative humidity (70-85%) during fruiting and frequent spraying of water is required in the cropping rooms depending upon the atmospheric humidity.

**Oyster mushroom**

The oyster mushroom can tolerate high carbon di oxide concentration during spawn run upto 2000 ppm while it should be less than 600 ppm during cropping. Light is required to initiate fruit body formation. Diffused light for one or two hours daily is sufficient. Inadequate light conditions can be judged by long stalk (stipe), small cap and poor yield. The optimum pH during substrate colonization should be between 6.0-7.0 while the pH of the water for spraying should be neither too acidic nor alkaline.

**Taxonomy**

| | | |
|---|---|---|
| *Kingdom* | : | *Fungi* |
| *Phylum* | : | *Basidiomycota* |
| *Subphylum* | : | *Basidiomycotina* |
| *Class* | : | *Agaricomycetes* |
| *Subclass* | : | *Agaricomycetidae* |
| *Order* | : | *Agaricales* |
| *Family* | : | *Pleurotaceae* |

**Varieties**

| | | |
|---|---|---|
| MDU 1 | : | *Pleurotus djamor* |
| MDU2 | : | *P. flabellatus* |
| CO 1 | : | *P.citrinopileatus* |
| *CO2* | : | *P.ostreatus* |
| APK 1 | : | *Peous* |

**3. Paddy Straw Mushroom: *Volvariella volvaceae, Volvariella diplasia***

This genus takes its name volva means a wrapper and which completely envelops the main fruiting body during the young stage. The fruit bodies of this mushroom first appear as greyish white buttons resembling a birds egg. At maturity the buttons enlarge and umbrella like fruit bodies emerge after the rupture of the volva. The basidiocarp of this mushroom has four distinct parts namely volva, stipe, pileus and gills. It takes 10-15 days for complete mycelial growth under optimum temperature conditions of 30-35°C.

**Paddy straw mushroom**

**Taxonomy**

| | | |
|---|---|---|
| *Kingdom* | : | *Fungi* |
| *Phylum* | : | *Basidiomycota* |
| *Subphylum* | : | *Basidiomycotina* |
| *Class* | : | *Agaricomycetes* |
| *Subclass* | : | *Agaricomycetidae* |
| *Order* | : | *Agaricales* |
| *Family* | : | *Pluteaceae* |

## 4. Milky Mushroom : *Calocybe indica*

Milky mushroom is an attractive white mushroom and its cultivation has become popular in Tamil Nadu on a commercial scale. This variety is tropical in nature and can be grown when button and oyster mushroom cannot be grown due to high temperature. It is cultivated in the growing temperature of 25-35°C and relative humidity of 70-85%

Milky mushroom

**Taxonomy**

| | | |
|---|---|---|
| *Kingdom* | : | *Fungi* |
| *Phylum* | : | *Basidiomycota* |
| *Subphylum* | : | *Basidiomycotina* |
| *Class* | : | *Agaricomycetes* |
| *Subclass* | : | *Agaricomycetidae* |
| *Order* | : | *Agaricales* |
| *Family* | : | *Lyophyllaceae* |

**Other cultivated mushrooms**

| | |
|---|---|
| Winter mushroom | *Flammulina velutipes* |
| Nameko mushroom | *Pholiota nameko* |
| Mu-Erb in Chinese<br>(Ear of trees) mushroom | *Auricularia auricula* |
| Jews ear mushroom<br>(Human ear) | *A. polytricha* |
| Shiitake mushroom | *Lentinus edodes* |
| White Jelly fungus or<br>Silver ear mushroom | *Tremella fuciformis* |

**Black ear mushroom**

## Ascomycota mushrooms

a. Morels - *Morchella* sp
*M.deliciosa, M.crussipes*
*M.esculenta, M.semilebra*
*M.angusticeps*

## Taxonomy

| | | |
|---|---|---|
| *Kingdom* | : | *Fungi* |
| *Phylum* | : | *Ascomycota* |
| *Class* | : | *Pezizomycetes* |
| *Order* | : | *Pezizales* |
| *Family* | : | *Morchellaceae* |

***Morchella mushroom***

b. Truffles - *Tuber* sp
*T.melanaspermum, T.aestivum, T.refum, T.mangatum*

**Taxonomy**

| | | |
|---|---|---|
| *Kingdom* | : | *Fungi* |
| *Phylum* | : | *Ascomycota* |
| *Class* | : | *Pezizomycetes* |
| *Order* | : | *Pezizales* |
| *Family* | : | *Tuberaceae* |

***Tuber Mushroom***

**Table 1 Comparison of different mushrooms**

| Character | Oyster mushroom | Button mushroom | Milky mushroom | Paddy straw mushroom |
|---|---|---|---|---|
| **Species** | *Pleurotus sp* | *Agaricus sp* | *Calocybe indica* | *Volvariella sp* |
| **Substrate** | Paddy straw | Compost | Paddy straw | Paddy straw |
| **Growing temperature** | 20-30°C | 15-25°C | 25-35°C | 30-35°C |
| **Crop cycle** | 30-45 days | 85-100 days | 45-50 days | 25-30 days |
| **Days for first harvest** | 10-25 days | 60-70 days | 24-28 days | 25-30 days |
| **Yield per bed** | 500g/bed | 3.5kg/bed | 356 g / bed | 5kg/bed |
| **Shelf life** | 1-3 days | 3-5 days | 3-5 days | 1-3 days |
| **Bio-efficiency** | 80-100% | 30-35% | 143% | 20-30% |

## Life cycle of Mushroom

The life cycle of *Pleurotus* sp. has been shown in Fig 2. On maturity, mushroom produces a number of spores which are released at intervals. The spores are dispersed by wind and germinate on a suitable medium to produce a primary mycelium. The cells of homokaryotic mycelium have only one type of nucleus, all being genetically identical. Mating between two compatible homokaryotic mycelia through hyphal fusion i.e., plasmogamy results in the formation of a heterokaryon and hence a fertile mycelium is obtained. The nuclear division and septum formation in this mycelium occurs through clamp connections.

Under appropriate environmental conditions the fertile mycelium produces fruit body. The spore bearing tissues of the fruit body produces columnar layer of club shaped binucleate cells called basidia. The paired nuclei in the basidia fuse (Karyogamy) to form the diploid nucleus.

Immediately meiosis occur and four haploid nuclei are formed which move to the basidiospore through stalk like structure called sterigmata. The basidiospores, so formed are discharged and again germination is initiated.

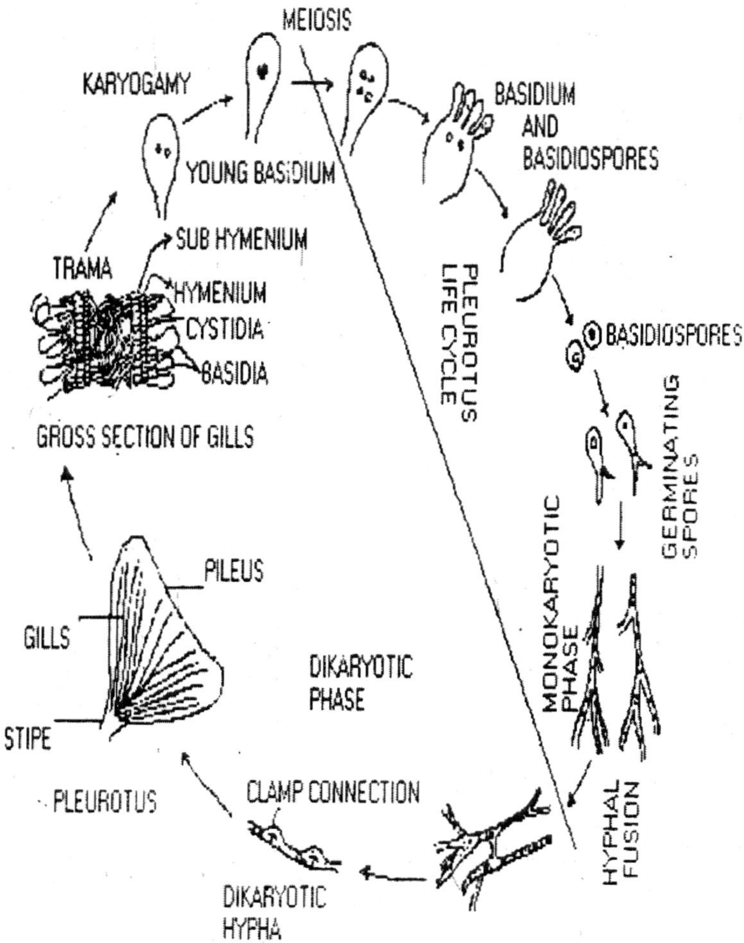


**Figure 2. The life cycle of Pleurotus sp**

## Identification of poisonous mushroom

Poisonous mushrooms are incapable of causing infectious diseases but produce toxic substances that poison a person who ingests them. These poisonous substances are collectively known as mycotoxins (myco = fungus + toxin = poison) and result in mycetismus (mushroom poisoning) following ingestion of poisonous mushrooms. These mushrooms contain lethal substances that destroy liver cells and excite the nervous system.

**Poisonous mushroom - *Amanita virosa***

The poisonous mushrooms have the toxic principle which is a mixture of á and â amanitin and phalloidin - both complex cyclic polypeptides containing sulfur. Cooking does not destroy the toxin nor the human digestive juices are affected it. Symptoms of poisoning appear only after 8-24 hours of ingestion and by time the toxin is absorbed by the body, neither vomiting nor a stomach pump can help then. Eating poisonous mushrooms may result in various types of reactions like nervous disorder, gastric disorder, haemolytic disorder and muscular disorder.

**Poisonous mushroom - *Boletus rubroflammeus***

**Guidelines for avoiding poisonous mushrooms**

- Avoid little brown mushroom (LBM) whose species can rarely be determined by amateurs
- Beware of mushrooms with a ring on its stalk
- *Amanita virosa* (destroying angel) - poisonous
- *Agaricus campestris* - edible (exception)

Beware of mushrooms with a sac or cup near the base of its stalk

- *Amanita phalloides (Death cap) - poisonous*
- *Amanita fulva edible - (*exception)

Beware of mushrooms with a swollen stalk

- *Amantia muscaria* – poisonous
- *Armillariella mellea* – edible (exception)

Beware of mushrooms with warts, setae or raised projections on its cap

- *Chlorophyllum molybdites, Amanita muscaria*
- (fly agaric)-poisonous
- *Lepiota procera*-edible (exception)
- Avoid all species *of Boletus*
- Avoid all brain like *(Gyromitra)*, saddle shaped *(Helvella)* fungi or deformed morels

- Never eat mushrooms whose inside are not pure white or undifferentiated.

**Beware of mushrooms growing on dung**

- Some *Coprinus* are poisonous and some of them are edible
- Beware of mushrooms, which turn silver spoon or silver coir black when they are dipped in a dish of poisonous mushroom
- Beware of mushrooms, which exude milky substances from damaged fruiting bodies
- Beware of mushrooms, which turn onion black on cooking
- Always use only known species of mushrooms for food purpose. It is advisable to check the edibility by taking a small quantity or feeding it to animals. Consuming alcohol after taking mushroom not advisable.

**Criteria suggested by mycologist for general classification is given below**

| Character | Edible mushroom | Poisonous mushroom |
|---|---|---|
| Colour | White or Gray | Ornamental |
| Scales | Absent | Present |
| Smell | Pleasant smell | Unpleasant smell |
| Cooking: | | |
| Using silver spoon | No change in the colour of spoon | Colour of spoon changes to black |
| Cooking with onion | No colour change in onion | Colour of onion changes to black |
| Presence of latex | Absent | Present |
| Presence of tough volva | Absent | Present |

# UNIT - 4
# SPAWN PRODUCTION TECHNIQUES OF EDIBLE MUSHROOMS

The isolation, purification and maintenance of mushroom culture require technical expertise and aseptic high-tech laboratory facilities. Successful mushroom production depends upon the proper maintenance of pure culture spawn that is capable of providing fruiting bodies of high productivity.

**Preparation of Potato Dextrose Agar Medium (PDA)**
**Media composition**

| | | |
|---|---|---|
| Peeled sliced potato pieces | : | 250 g |
| Dextrose | : | 20g |
| Agar Agar | : | 20 g |
| pH | : | 7.0 |
| Distilled water | : | 1 litre |

The potatoes are peeled, washed, and cut into pieces. They are cooked in 500 ml water for half an hour to one hour. In the same way 20 g of agar is melted in another 500 ml of water by heating in a pressure cooker. The boiled potato juice and the melted agar are filtered through a sieve into a one litre measuring cylinder. Glucose (20 g) is added to the filtered juice. The pH is adjusted to 7 (Above pH-7 Add few drops of 0.1 N hydrochloric acid, below pH-7 - Add few drops of 0.1 N sodium hydroxide). One hundred ml of this medium is distributed equally in each conical flask, The mouth of the conical flask is plugged with non-absorbent cotton and covered with a piece of paper and tied with a thread. The conical flask containing the medium is then autoclaved at 15 lb pressure for 20 minutes.

**Preparation of Oat Meal Agar Medium (OMA)**

This medium is prepared as that of PDA

**Media composition**

| | | |
|---|---|---|
| Oat meal | : | 40g |
| Agar agar | : | 20g |
| Distilled water | : | 1 litre |
| pH | : | 7.0 |

**Isolation of mushroom is done by tissue culture technique**

**Tissue culture technique**

Fresh mushroom is collected and swabbed with 80 per cent ethyl alcohol for surface sterilization. The mushroom is cut at the junction of pileus and stipe with sterile blade and the tissue bits taken with a sterile forceps and placed on sterilized Petri plates containing 10ml of 2 per cent sodium hypochloride for one minute or in 0.1 percent mercuric chloride for 30 seconds. Subsequently the tissues are serially washed twice in sterile distilled water to get rid of sodium hypochlorite or mercuric chloride. Then the tissues are kept on the centre of the Petri plate containing PDA or OMA medium. The plates are incubated at room temperature for 7 days. Pure white mycelial growth will be observed radiating from the centre of the medium, A small bit of pure growth of mushroom fungus is to be transferred to an agar slant and maintained as mother culture. This can be subcultured once in three months (Fig. 3).

**Mother Culture of mushroom**

## Mother spawn preparation

Mushroom mycelium i.e. pure culture of the mushroom fungus used for cultivating mushroom is known as 'spawn'. The first generation fungal culture is called the mother spawn'. The mother spawn can be successfully used upto third or fourth commercial spawn (Bed spawn) for mushroom cultivation. After fourth generation it might loose its efficiency.

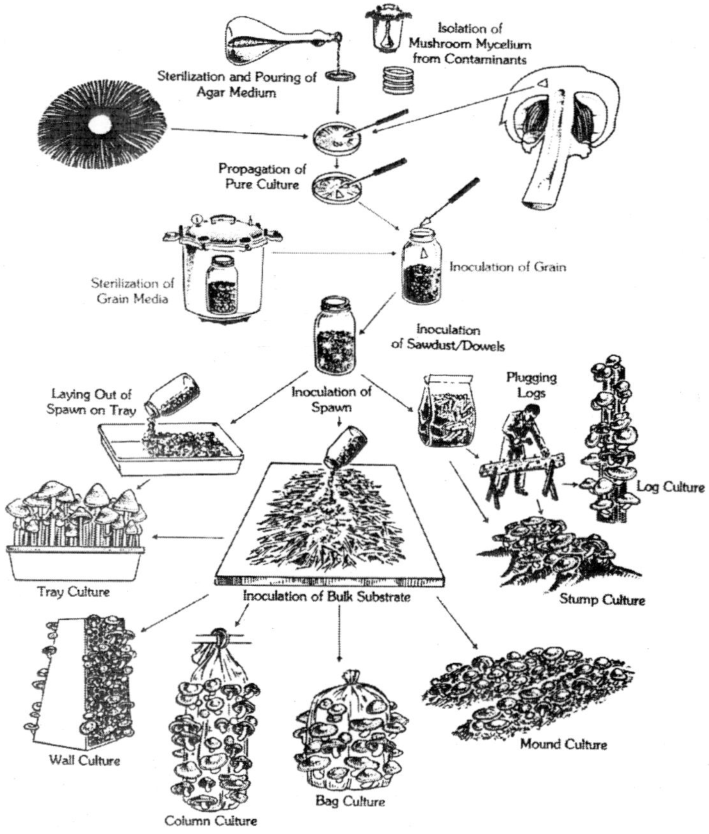


**Figure 3. Tissue Culture Technique**

The cholam (Sorghum), grains (1 kg) are placed in a trough of water to remove the chaffy grains. Then they are half cooked (approximately 30 minutes). The excess water is drained and spread over a clean sack or hessian cloth. The sack or hessian cloth can be dipped in fungicide solution containing 5 g carbendazim or 10g thiram or mancozeb dissolved in 10 litres of water. For every kg of grains 20 g calcium carbonate is mixed so as to maintain the pH for the growth of the fungus.

Moreover, the calcium carbonate coating prevents the grains from sticking. These grains are filled in polypropylene bags (30 x 12 cm and 150 guage thickness). Then the bags are tightly plugged with non-absorbent cotton, pvc pipe ring and wrapped with a paper, tied with a thread and placed in an autoclave for sterilization (20 lb pressure for 2 hours). After cooling, the bags are ready for inoculation. (Instead of cholam grains, wheat grains, paddy grains, ill filled paddy grains etc can be used).

**Inoculation technique**

The sterilized bottles are taken into the culture room. This is a close room with an ordinary fluorescent tube light and an ultra violet lamp. The ultra violet lamp is switched on for 15 minutes to sterilize the air inside. Then it is switched off and the ordinary fluorescent tube light is switched on the inoculation work can also be done in the Laminar Flow Chamber

With the help of the cork borer a 10 mm diameter disc is made from the Petri plates living fully grown mushroom fungus. Four to five 10mm fungal discs are transferred into the sterilized spawn bags with the help of an inoculation needle. This is done over the Bunsen burner (near the flame to avoid contamination. The bottles are incubated at room temperature. In about 15 days, growth of white mushroom mycelium is observed in the entire bags. This is known as 'mother spawn' (Fig.3).

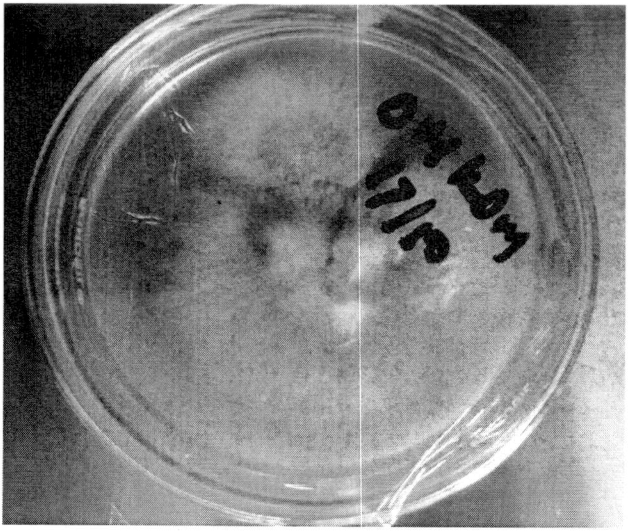


**Pure culture of mushroom**

**Multiplication of spawn from mother spawn**

From a single mother spawn, 30 spawn bags could be prepared. The calcium carbonate mixed grains are sterilized as per the above method. The sterilized bottles are inoculated using the mother spawn. Two persons are required to transfer the inoculum from the mother spawn. One person should hold the mother spawn bag in his left hand and open the cotton plug with right hand by keeping the mouth of the bag near the flame. The second person now can open the sterilized bag with cholam grains in the same way holding the cotton plug in the right hand. Now, the first person holding the mother spawn bag should transfer about 10 g of cholam grains along with the mushroom fungus to the new bag. The inoculated bag is plugged with the non absorbant cotton immediately and wrapped with paper and tied with a thread. The spawn bag is incubated for 15 days for spawn run. Spawn when stored under normal room temperature can be used up to a maximum period of 30 days from the date of inoculation.

**Spawn bottles**

**Spawn room**

## Types of spawn

### Natural spawn or Virgin spawn

This is termed as natural spawn because it occurs under natural conditions of environment and never been propagated artificially. The soil containing the spawn underneath clumps of mushrooms was collected and used. One of the methods of obtaining natural spawn is to collect horse droppings all along the highways during the summer, mixing it with some road sand and piling it in a dry shed. The manure obtained in this way should not be allowed to heat above 100°F and should have proper moisture content or else the spores will die.

### Mill-track spawn

"Mill-track" spawn originated from the spawn found in covered road ways at mills or along tram-car-tracks where horses were used. The accumulation of manure is sometime mixed with saw-dust or earth which provides a congenial atmosphere for mycelial establishment.

### Brick-spawn

The brick spawn is so called because the material in which the mycelium is present in the form of bricks. These bricks are about 5 x 8 x 1½ inches in size.

### Method of preparation

Equal parts of horse dung, and cowdung, and loam soil are thoroughly mixed together to a consistency of mortar. This is pressed in the form of bricks and dried. These bricks are piled upon a layer of fresh horse manure about 8 inches deep, the pile of bricks being about 3 feet height. This pile is then covered over loosely with fresh horse manure (temperature below $100^{0}$F). They are left in this condition unit) the mycelium has thoroughly permeated the bricks. The spawn is completed and put upon the market. This type of spawn was manufactured in England eg: Barter spawn.

### Flake spawn or French spawn

It is extensively manufactured in France. The bed is spawned in the ordinary way. When the mycelium has thoroughly permeated the bed, it is taken and broken into irregular pieces, six to eight inches in diameter. This is entirely of horse manure with no admixture of soil.

# UNIT - 5
# CULTIVATION OF OYSTER MUSHROOM

The oyster mushroom is one of the most suitable fungal organisms for producing protein rich food from agro wastes without composting. It can be easily cultivated on any of the agro waste without composting. It can be easily cultivated on any of the agricultural wastes containing lignin and cellulose, It does not require complicated substrates preparation as in *Agaricus bisporus* and can be grown in non fermented, almost fresh plant residues.

Its substrate preparation technique is very simple. Moreover, it does not require controlled environmental conditions like *Agaricus bisporus* for cultivation. One can harvest a minimum of about 500 kg fresh oyster Mushroom from 1 tonne of dry wheat or paddy straw in 45-60 days, while with the same quantity of straw only about 200 kg of white button mushrooms are obtained in 100-200 days. The initial investment as well as cost of production is very low, as costly equipments like boiler and controlled cropping rooms are not required.

The bodies of this mushroom are distinctly shell, fan or spatula shaped with different shades of white, cream, grey, yellow, pink or light brown depending upon the species. However, the colour of the sporophores are extremely variable character influenced by the temperature, light intensity and nutrient of the substrate.

## Cultivation technology

The paddy straw is cut into small bits (3-5cm) and soaked in a cement trough for about 1-2 hours. The water is drained and the pre soaked straw is transferred to a G.I drum or any metallic vessel and water is added. The straw is boiled for 30 minutes. Again the water is drained and the straw is spread on a clean sack or hessian cloth previously soaked in fungicide solution (carbendazim) or potassium pemanganate solution (19/1). The straw is shade dried. It should contain optimum moisture (60-65%) by adopting squeeze method. Low moisture content in the straw will not permit proper spawn run. One kg of dry paddy straw when boiled and shade dried will approximately weigh two kg.

**Oyster mushroom**

## Squeeze method

Take a handful of wet paddy straw and squeeze it in between hand. Water droplets should not come out from hand. Further, water droplets should not present on palm and in between fingers.

Polythene bag of 60x30 cm size is taken and two holes of one cm diameter are made in the centre to ensure aeration. The bottom of the polythene bag is tied with a thread to provide a flat circular bottom to the mushroom beds. The spawn bag is taken and with the help of a sterilized iron hook the mushroom spawn is dug out and placed on a clean plastic tray. The spawn from a bag is divided into two halves and can be used for preparing two mushroom beds. Each half of the spawn is further divided into five parts.

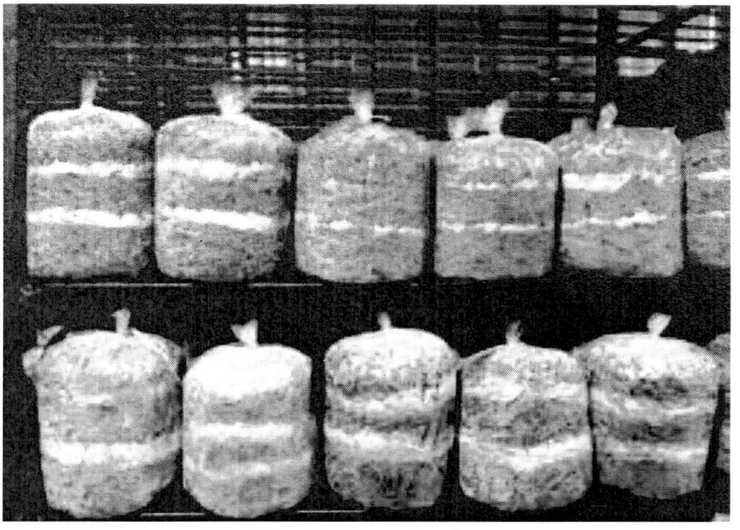

**Mushroom beds**

The straw bits are uniformly placed at the bottom of polythene bags to a height of about five cm. One portion of the spawn(Out of the five parts) is sprinkled over the entire surface of the straw. The second layer of straw is spread over the first layer to a height of 10 cm. Then the second part of the spawn is sprinkled over the entire surface of the straw. Then the third layer of the straw is spread over the second layer to a height of 10 cm and the third portion of the spawn is sprinkled over the entire third layer of straw.

Then the fourth layer of straw is spread over the third layer to a height of 10 cm and the fourth portion of the spawn is sprinkled over the entire surface of the fourth layer. Finally the fifth portion of the spawn is sprinkled over the fourth layer of straw. Then it is covered with bits of straw to a height of five cm and the top of the polythene bag is tied with a thread. The polythene bag is gently jerked as and when the straw is spread to get a uniform filling of straw and a typical cylindrical shaped bed.

The prepared cylindrical beds are kept in a spawn running room of the mushroom shed. Spawn running will be completed in about 10 to 20 days (as per the variety used)

**Mushroom shed**

Mushroom shed should be preferably thatched. It should have à door. The thatched portions can be covered with chicken mesh to prevent entry of snakes, rats and squirrels. The floor of the shed may be filled with sand to a height of 30 cm and watered. Racks are to be erected inside the mushroom house to accommodate the mushroom beds. The inner side of the mushroom shed can be lined with gunny bags and watered twice daily to keep the room cool. The shed may be laid in East - West to avoid direct effect of sun and to reduce the temperature inside the cropping room, Cropping room should have diffused light and good ventilation (Fig.4).

**Table 2 Approximate space requirement of cropping and spawn running room**

| S. No. | Expected mushroom production | Size of spawn running room | Size of cropping room | No. of beds per day | No. of racks (80 beds / racks) |
|---|---|---|---|---|---|
| 1 | 1 kg | 8 $m^2$ (4 x 2m) | 8 $m^2$ (4 x 2 m) | 4 | 2 |
| 2 | 5 kg | 40.5 $m^2$ (13.5 x 3m) | 40.5 $m^2$ (13.5 x 3m) | 20 | 10 |
| 3 | 20 kg | 162 $m^2$ (27 x 6 m) | 162 $m^2$ (27 x 6 m) | 80 | 40 |

| | | |
|---|---|---|
| Size of the door | : | 2 m height x 0.76 m width |
| Size of the ventilator | : | 0.60 x 0.30 m |
| No. of ventilators | : | 2 to12 |

**Approximate size of rack for cropping room**

| | | |
|---|---|---|
| Length | : | 2.5 m |
| Height | : | 2.25 m |
| Breadth | : | 0.6 m |
| No. of tiers | : | 4 |
| Height between 2 tiers | : | 0.45 m |
| Clearance from ground level for bottom tier | : | 0.4 m |
| Capacity of rack | : | 80 beds |
| Air bed ratio | : | 1 : 8 |

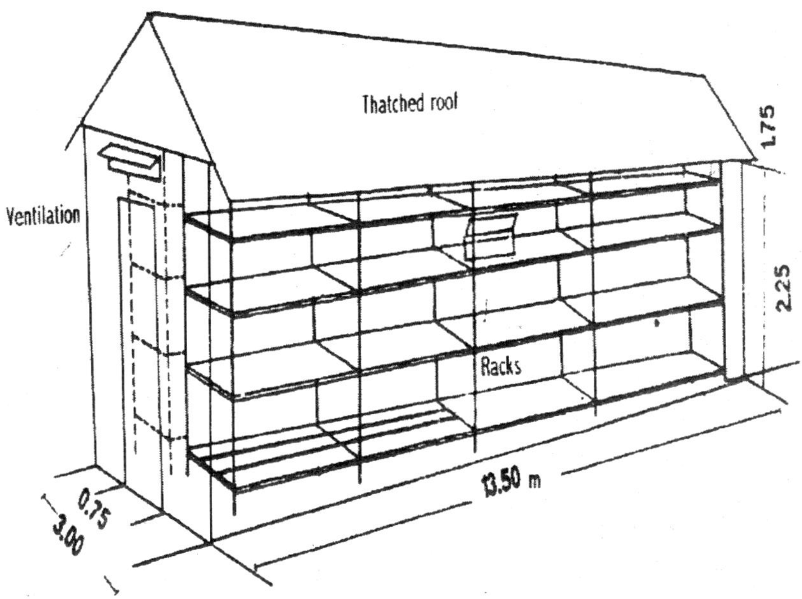


**Figure 4. Mushroom Shed**

## Spawn running room

Spawn running room is one where the beds are kept for spawn running. Proliferation of mushroom fungus mycelium in and on the beds is called spawn running. An ordinary room or thatched shed can be used as a spawn running room. Multi tier racks can be provided in the room to have more space. Beds may be arranged in one or two rows in each tier. This room needs ventilation and diffused sun light. Temperature in the room should be 24 to 28°C. Spawn running will be completed in about 10 to 20 days (as per the variety used)

## Cropping room

Cropping room is one where the opened mushroom beds are kept after completion of spawn running. This room requires relatively cooler temperature than spawn running room. The temperature should be 23 to 25$^{0}$C. Most of the growers use the same room for spawn running and cropping. In plains, floor of the shed may be filled with sand to a height of 30cm. All the sides should be closed with thatching material inner side should be lined with hanging gunny. The floor and the gunny should be wet with water twice a day. Minimum 4-6 ventilators with fly proof net are needed. Length and breadth can be modified as per convenience. Cropping room should have diffused light and good ventilation.

The polythene bag is opened by cutting with a sterile blade on 10$^{th}$ day of spawning for while oyster Mushroom (opening dates differ as per variety) and kept in the cropping room. The moisture level of the beds are observed and watered accordingly. The mushroom beds with excess moisture will lead to contamination. Pin heads appear on third or fourth day of opening of the beds and fully grown mushroom appear within three to four days of appearance of pin heads.

The mushroom should be harvested early morning before watering the bed. After the first harvest is completed the beds are scrapped one to two cm deep from the entire surface of the bed. The second crop appears within another week. Three to four crops of mushroom can be had in this way from a single bed. The entire cropping will be over in about 35-40 days for white oyster mushroom (days differ as per variety). The shelf life is about 12-16 hours at room temperature (differs as per varicty).

### Cultivation of APK *1, Pleurotus eous*

Cultivation aspects are similar to *Pleurotus* sp. except the number of holes in the polythene bags. For *P. eous* mushroom more number of holes (8-9 / polythene) should be made. It takes about 8-10 days for spawn run and the entire cropping will he over in about 30 days. The mushroom is initially dark pink and takes pink shade during maturity. Due to the high fibre content, it's keeping quality is increased and can be stored for 3 days under room temperature.

**Grown oyster mushroom**

# UNIT - 6
# CULTIVATION OF MILKY MUSHROOM

All the mushroom varieties released from TNAU namely APK 1, MDU 1, MDU2, CO 1 and Ooty 1 are belong to *Pleurotus* sp, whereas milky mushroom belongs to entirely different species namely *Calocybe indica and Macrocybe* sp.

**Special Features**

**Attractive colour and shape**

This mushroom is umbrella shaped and resemble button mushroom. The sporophore are robust, attractive and milky white in colour.

**Milky mushroom**

**Easy to cultivate**

The cultivation technology is very simple as that of *Pleurotus* sp.

**Suitable climate**

Under this, milky mushroom grows well at temperature range of 25-35$^0$C and RH 75-80%; it can be cultivated throughout the year in almost all districts of Tamil Nadu.

### More yield

Mean yield is 356g/ bed (which contain: 250g of paddy straw on dry weight basis) and accounts to 143% bio efficiency.

### Short duration

Mushroom can be harvested from 24-28 days after spawning and total crop cycle is 45-50 days when compared to button mushroom; this is shorter in duration.

### More weight mushroom

An average of single mushroom weighs about 55-60 g; sometimes more weight of 472 g/mushroom has been recorded.

### Increased shelf life

The storage of mushroom is 3-5days under normal condition, This mushroom is highly suitable for drying and canning, soup powder preparation and pickle making.

### Protein and fibre rich food

Protein content of milky mushroom is 32.3% and crude fibre content is 41%.

### Attractive market price

In market, mushroom fetches Rs. 200-250/kg, while oyster and button mushroom sold for Rs.150-200/kg and 200-250/kg respectively.

### Cultivation techniques

Milky mushroom can be cultivated on wide range of cellulosic substrates namely paddy straw, maize stalk, sorghum, pearl millet stalk, palmarosa grass, vettiver grass, sugarcane bagasse, soyabean meal and groundnut shell.

## Cultivation chamber

Beds after preparation may be kept under normal room temperature (25-35$^0$C) for spawn run, after completion of spawn run and after casing the beds are to be incubated over racks in partially sunken chamber lined with blue coloured HDP sheet as roofing material. Inside the chamber the temperature should be around 30-35$^0$C and RH >85%, High intensity of about 1600-3200 lux is essential in cropping room. Proper ventilation for gaseous exchange is also essential.

## Mushroom bed preparation

Polythene bags of 60 x 30cm size are used for mushroom bed. Chopped paddy straw bits (3-5 cm) are soaked in cold water for 4 hrs. After draining the excess water, straw bits are boiled for 30-40 min in separate drum. Straw can be used for bed preparation after excess moisture drained. At the time of bed preparation, the substrate containing around 65% moisture (squeeze method) sorghum/paddy chaff spawn may be used. Cylindrical beds are prepared following layer method of spawning as done in the case of oyster mushroom, each bag of spawn, 2 cylindrical beds are prepared. The beds are incubated under semi dark condition in a clean room. Spawn running would be completed in 10-12days.

**Milky mushroom beds**

## Casing

Unlike oyster mushroom cultivation, milky mushroom involves additional process called casing, After the completion of spawn running, the cylindrical beds are cut horizontally into two equal parts. Over each half casing soil is applied to height of 1-2 cm. For casing garden soil or clay loam is sterilized (20 lb pressure for 2 hour) and pH should be around 7. In some cases, red soil is mixed with sand and $CaCO_3$, (2%), any other porous mediumn with good water holding capacity, moderate cation exchange capacity and low electrical conductivity are also be used.

**Milky mushroom**

## Cropping

Beds after casing are kept in cultivation chamber and sprayed regularly with water to maintain 60% moisture level in casing medium. Pin heads appear in 8-10 days after casing and first harvest can be made in 6-8 days after pin head formation.

Mushroom should be harvested before they start shedding the spores. After taking the first harvest, casing medium is gently ruffled, slightly compacted back and sprayed regularly with water second and third harvest may be obtained within 45-50 days of bed preparation. The harvested beds are removed. and fresh beds may be kept for cropping.

### Yield

Mean yield is 356 g/bed. Bioefficiency is 143%. The average mnushroom weight of single mushroom is 55-60 g and sometimes a maximum of 472 g.

### Nutritive value

| | | |
|---|---|---|
| Moisture | - | 85.58% |
| Crude ash | - | 8.89% |
| Crude protein | - | 32.29% |
| Crude fibre | - | 41.10% |
| Crude fat | - | 0.67% |
| Total Carbohydrate | - | 9.85% |
| Iron | – | 0.08% |
| Ca | – | 0.12% |
| P | – | 0.8% |
| Na | – | 0.95% |
| K | – | 4.92% |

Because of its increased fibre content, this mushroom serves as diet to persons suffering from peptic ulcers, constipation and human ailments. Protein and carbohydrate available are present in easily digestible manner.

# UNIT - 7
# CULTIVATION OF BUTTON MUSHROOM

*Agaricus bisporus*, a temperate mushroom can grow best only under temperate condition and 24°C is the optimum temperature. It generally produces a basidiocarp with a white to brown or grey brown cap, free gills, an annulus but no vulva and a stalk that readily separates from the cap.

Like other fungi, *Agaricus bisporus* is a heterotrophic organism. It requires carbon compounds that have already been formed by green plants (autotrophs). Besides carbon, it requires nitrogen, essential elements such as phosphorus, sulfur, potassium and iron; vitamins such as thiamine and biotin. All the ingredients that contain these compounds are mixed in a fixed proportion and fermented in a set pattern to form a substrate, which is known as compost. Some of the compost formulations suggested are given below:

**Button mushroom**

**Formulae given by I.A.R.I., New Delhi**

| | | | |
|---|---|---|---|
| **I.** | Horse manure | : | 1000 kg |
| | Wheat straw | : | 350 kg |
| | Urea | : | 3 kg |
| | Gypsum | : | 30-40 kg |

| | | | |
|---|---|---|---|
| **II.** | Horse manure | : | 1000 kg |
| | Wheat straw | : | 500 kg |
| | Chicken manure | : | 300 kg |
| | Brewer's grain | : | 60 kg |
| | Urea | : | 7 kg |
| | Gypsum | : | 30 kg |

**Formulae given by Punjab Agricultural University, Ludhiana**

| | | | |
|---|---|---|---|
| **I.** | Wheat and paddy straw (1:1) | : | 300 kg |
| | Calcium ammonium nitrate | : | 9 kg |
| | Urea | : | 3 kg |
| | Super phosphate | : | 3 kg |
| | Muriate of Potash | : | 3 kg |
| | Wheat bran | : | 15 kg |
| | Molasses | : | 5 kg |
| | Gypsum | : | 30 kg |
| | Insecticide | : | 250 g |

| | | | |
|---|---|---|---|
| **II.** | Wheat straw | : | 300 kg |
| | Poultry litter | : | 60 kg |
| | Calcium ammonium nitrate | : | 6 kg |
| | Superphosphate | : | 3 kg |
| | Wheat bran | : | 15 kg |
| | Gypsum | : | 30 kg |
| | Insecticide | : | 250 g |

**Formulae given by N.C.M.R., Solan**

| | | | |
|---|---|---|---|
| **I.** | Wheat straw | : | 300 kg |
| | Wheat bran | : | 15 kg |
| | Chicken manure | : | 125 kg |
| | Urea | : | 5.5 kg |
| | Gypsum | : | 20 kg |
| | Insecticide | : | 125 g |

| | | | |
|---|---|---|---|
| **II.** | Wheat and paddy straw (1 :1) | : | 300 kg |
| | Calcium ammonium nitrate | : | 9 kg |
| | Urea | : | 4 kg |
| | Wheat bran | : | 25 kg |
| | Gypsum | : | 20 kg |
| | Insecticide | : | 125 g |

**Long method**

| | | | |
|---|---|---|---|
| **I.** | Wheat straw | : | 1 tonne |
| | Calcium ammonium nitrate | : | 30 kg |
| | Super phosphate | : | 25 kg |
| | Urea | : | 12 kg |
| | Sulphate of potash | : | 10 kg |
| | Wheat bran | : | 100 kg |
| | Molasses | : | 16.6 litres |
| | Gypsum | : | 100 kg |

**Short method**

| | | |
|---|---|---|
| Wheat straw | : | 1000 kg |
| Chicken manure | : | 400 kg |
| Brewer's manure | : | 72 kg |
| Urea | : | 14.5 kg |
| Gypsum | : | 30 kg |

**Formulae given by I.I.H.R., Bangalore**

| | | | |
|---|---|---|---|
| **I.** | Paddy straw | : | 150 kg |
| | Maize stalks | : | 150 kg |
| | Ammonium sulphate | : | 9 kg |
| | Super phosphate | : | 9 kg |
| | Urea | : | 4 kg |
| | Rice bran | : | 50 kg |
| | Cotton seed meal | : | 5 kg |
| | Gypsum | : | 12 kg |
| | Calcium carbonate | : | 10 kg |

| | | | |
|---|---|---|---|
| **II.** | Wheat straw or | : | 300 kg |
| | Paddy straw | : | 400 kg |
| | Calcium ammonium nitrate | : | 9 kg |
| | Super phosphate | : | 9 kg |
| | Urea | : | 4 kg |
| | Wheat bran | : | 30 kg |
| | Gypsumn | : | 12 kg |
| | Calcium carbonate | : | 10 kg |
| **III.** | Wheat straw | : | 300 kg |
| | Chicken manure | : | 120 kg |
| | Rice bran | : | 20.6 kg |
| | Brewer's grain | : | 22 kg |
| | Urea | : | 6 kg |
| | Cotton seed meal | : | 5 kg |
| | Gypsum | : | 10 kg |
| **IV.** | Paddy straw | : | 3 tonnes |
| | Chicken manure | : | 1.5 tonnes |
| | Wheat bran | : | 125 kg |
| | Gypsum | : | 90 kg |

**Formulae given by I.C.A.R. Research Complex, Shillong**

| | | | |
|---|---|---|---|
| **I.** | Paddy straw | : | 400 kg |
| | Ammoniun sulphate | : | 9 kg |
| | Urea | : | 3.6 kg |
| | Molasses | : | 5.0 kg |
| | Sulphate of potash | : | 3 kg |
| | Single super phosphate | : | 3 kg |
| | Wheat bran | : | 30 kg |
| | Gypsum | : | 30 kg |
| | Insecticide | : | 250 g |

**Formulae given by RRL., Srinagar**

| | | | |
|---|---|---|---|
| **I.** | Wheat bran | : | 300 kg |
| | Molasses | : | 12 kg |
| | Urea | : | 4.5 kg |
| | Wheat bran | : | 50 kg |
| | Muriate of Potash | : | 2 kg |
| | Cotton seed meal | : | 5 kg |
| | Gypsum | : | 15 kg |
| **II.** | Paddy straw | : | 300 kg |
| | Molasses | : | 12 kg |
| | Urea | : | 6 kg |
| | Wheat bran | : | 50 kg |
| | Muriate of Potash | : | 2 kg |
| | Cotton seed meal | : | 5 kg |
| | Gypsum | : | 25 kg |

**Formulae given by T.N.A.U., Coimbatore**

| | | |
|---|---|---|
| Paddy straw | : | 100 kg |
| Urea | : | 1 kg |
| Calcium ammonium nitrate | : | 2 kg |
| Super phosphate | : | 2 kg |
| Calcium carbonate | : | 2.5 kg |
| Rice bran | : | 5 kg |
| Gypsum | : | 3 kg |

**Table 3 Composition of raw materials after decomposition (Gerrits 1988)**

| | | | | | Kg/tonne of dry material | | |
|---|---|---|---|---|---|---|---|
| Ingredients | % Moisture | Organic material | Nitrogen (N) | Phosporic acid ($P_2O_5$) | Potassium ($K_2O$) | Calcium (Ca) | Magnesium (MgO) |
| Wheat Straw | 15 | 918 | 54 | 24 | 10.1 | 2.6 | 1.4 |
| Horse manure | 63 | 840 | 13 | 4 | 18 | 8 | 2 |
| Chicken droppings | 40 | 810 | 45 | 41 | 37 | 35 | 10 |
| Urban compost | 50 | 400 | 10 | 3.3 | 16 | 56 | 4.9 |
| Grass, hay | 15 | 930 | 18 | 9.8 | 36 | 7.7 | 2.7 |
| Lucerne hay | 15 | 930 | 28 | 6.6 | 30 | 27 | 4.6 |
| Cotton waste | 9 | 910 | 65 | 22 | 15 | 4.5 | 8.5 |
| Ammonium Sulphate | 0 | 0 | 220 | 0 | 0 | 0 | 0 |
| Urea | 0 | 0 | 640 | 0 | 0 | 0 | 0 |
| Chalk | 20 | 0 | 0 | 0 | 0 | 325 | 0 |

## 1. Preparation of compost

Basically there are three methods of composting. These are as follows:

a. Long method of composting
b. Short method of composting
c. Indoor composting

### a. Long method of composting (LMC)

This method of composting was first advocated in India by Mantel *et al.* (1972).

The compost should be prepared on clean concrete floor in the composting yard. Size of the composting yard depends upon the size of the mushroom farm. Composting yard having a platform of 100'x 40' is sufficient enough to accommodate compost for 400-500 trays (30-40 kg/tray). Composting can also be done in open space but there should be some provision to protect the pile from rains. Compost should be covered with polythene sheet during rainy period.

To begin the composting process, clean the composting yard or the space where compost is to be prepared thoroughly and wash it with 2% formalin solution. Wheat straw or any other base material to be used is spread on the floor upto the height of 9"-12". Wet the straw thoroughly by spraying water and turning the straw with the help of iron forks. There should be ample supply of water during the phase of composting. Proper wetting will require about 4-5 times watering. When the straw is completely wet, it is kept as such for 24 h. Similarly all the fertilizers including chicken manure and wheat bran are mixed together and water is sprinkled over them so that they become moist. Later on, this mixture is covered with moist gunny bag.

Day-0: On this day, the fertilizer mixtures are spread on the wet wheat straw and mixed thoroughly with the help of iron forks. This mixture is made into stack with the help of iron or wooden boards. Small quantity of water is regularly sprinkled to wet dry portions while the pile is made. Dimensions of the pile should be 5'x5'x length. Height and width of the pile should not be more than that; otherwise, pile may become too hot due to high temperature or anaerobic conditions may prevail in the centre which may not yield good quality compost. The stack is generally made with the help of iron or wooden boards, three in number representing 2 sideboards and one end. For making the stack or heap compost ingredients are put in the mould is completely filled with the composting materials sideboards are moved lengthwise and again filled up with the ingredients. In this manner, a long pile can be formed.

**Day 1-5:** Prepared pile is kept as such for 5 days. Temperature of the heap start rising and should reach 65-70 °C after 24-48 hours. Temperature built up in the pile depends upon several factors *viz.,* availability of carbohydrates, built up of micro flora, dimension of the pile and amount of nitrogen used in the mixture. Maintaining a proper temperature inside the stack is an important parameter of compost preparation. During this stage if it is felt that moisture in the compost pile is less, then more water can be added. Watering should be stopped as soon as leaching, starts from this bottom of the pile. If large quantity of water is leaching then the same may be collected and poured on the top of pile as the same contains different nutrients required for composting.

**Compost preparation**

**Day-6(First turning)**: On this day first turning is given to the stack. The aim of turning is that every portion of the pile gets equal aeration and water for proper decomposition of the base material. If the turning is not given to the stack, anaerobic conditions may prevail in the pile which ultimately leads to non selective compost. Turnings are given in such a manner that each and every portion of the stack is reshuffled and mixed properly. Stack is exposed to air and one may find different temperatures, in different zones of the stack. In the stack, central portion is fermenting and has maximum temperature. Rest of the portion is either fermenting partially or not at all. The correct method of turning is as follows. Remove about 1 ft of compost from top and side of the pile, shake them thoroughly so that excess of ammonia is released and it is exposed to air properly, keep this portion on one side, Now remove the central and bottom portion of the pile, shake these with the forks and keep them separately. Now a new pile is made with the help of boards indicated above keeping central portion at the bottom. Top and side portions should be placed at the centre while bottom part comes on top and sides. During pile formation watering is done if required.

**Day - 10 (Second turning)**: Pile is opened and turned as discussed earlier; water may be added if required.

**Day 13 (Third turning):** Again turning is given and required quantity of gypsum is added and restacked.

**Day 16 (Fourth turning)**: 400 g of furadon 3 g/ton of straw is added to check the nematodes.

**Day 19: (Fifth turning)**

**Day 22 : (Sixth turning)**

**Day 25: (Seventh turning):** Required quantity of Insecticide is added during turning.

**Day 28 (Filling day):** Pile is break opened and checked for ammonia smell. If no ammonia smell is there in the compost and a sweet smell is coming out, compost is ready and can be used for cultivation. If slight ammonia smell persists, then an additional turning can be given immediately. Normally ammonia concentration at spawning should not be more than 8-10 ppm. Correct amount of ammonia present in the compost can be measured with the help of drag or tubes available in the market. By this method compost preparation takes around 28-30 days for its completion. In this procedure considerable amount of dry matter is lost (around 40%).

**Attributes of a good compost**

- A good compost should be dark brown in colour
- It should not be greasy or sticky
- It should have distinctive sweet inoffensive smell
- There should not be any smell of ammonia
- It should have 68-70% moisture
- pH of the compost should be in the range of 7.2-7.8
- There should not be any visible growth of other undesirable organisms execpt for the fire fangs
- It should be free from insects and nematodes.

**b. Short method of composting (SMC)**

Long method of composting as described above has many shortcomings as it is a total outdoor procedure, where pasteurization is not affected and therefore, it is liable to be infested with number of pests and disease, ultimately reducing the yields. Maximum yield obtained by long method tends to be between 8-10 kg/100kg of compost. This method of composting is prevailing only in India, and in some developing countries where as it has been discarded long back from the advanced countries. To overcome above shortcomings Sinden and Hauser (1950,1953) came out with the novel method which is termed as short method of composting in which the compost is ready in about 16-20 days as compared to 28 days in long method. Further, compost obtained by such a method is free from the diseases and pests and gives 15-20 kg mushrooms/ 100 kg of compost. Short method of composting primarily consists of two phases: outdoor composting for 10-12 days (Phase-I) followed by pasteurization and conditioning of the compost inside an insulated room by free circulation of air under definite set of conditions (Phase II). This phase lasts for around seven days. This method of composting was introduced in India by Hayes and Shandilaya(1977).

**Outdoor composting (Phase I)**

Under this phase, all the ingredients are allowed to ferment under uncontrolled conditions for 10-12 days. This brings about the partial decomposition of the straw. Heat is generated in the processes which results in the rise in temperature to 70-80°C in the central zone where certain chemical process set free which results in caramelization of carbon compounds which give distinct brown colour to the compost.

In the outer zone temperature remains in the range of 50 60°C, where huge population of thermophilic flora develop. This serves as the inoculum for undecomposed compost.

**Day (-4):** On this day preliminary low stack is prepared with thoroughly wet wheat straw chicken manure and brewers grain which is trampled hard to make it anaerobic.

**Day (-2):** Stack is break opened and sufficient water is added especially to dry patches and again an anaerobic stack is made.

**Day 1**: On this date the stack is again break opened, full quantity of other raw materials is added, water is also added if required and anaerobic stack is made. Tunings can be done manually or by compost turners built for the purpose.

**Day 2:** First turning is given

**Day 4:** Second turning

**Day 6**: Third turning and gypsum is added.

**Day 8:** The compost is ready for the pasteurization (Phase II)

**Pasteurization (Phase II)**

**Peak heating**: Temperature of the room is kept within the range of 48-60°C. There should be free circulation of air and oxygen supply should be between 15-20% for proper development of the thermophilic flora. All this is done in a well insulated room in trays. To pasteurize 250 trays, a room of 24' x 15x12' (LxWxH) will be sufficient, keeping proper air and steam circulation in mind. To start the procedure, first the peak heating room is heated with dry heat to bring the temperature of the room 48.8°C. After that compost from Phase I is immediately transferred in this room to minimize the heat losses in transit. All the doors and ventilators are closed and fan is switched on to have uniform distribution of air for two hours, fresh air also introduced for a short while. On the second day live steam is introduced in the room to raise the temperature to 48-52°C for 4 days. This temperature is maintained for 2-4 days. After that fresh air is introduced for 15-20 minutes. Then all the doors and ventilators are closed and the steam is injected to raise the temperature to 58-60°C for 4 hours. Steam supply is then cut off and fresh air is gradually introduced in the room to lower the temperature in the room. Temperature is maintained for the conditioning of the compost. During this period the compost is free from ammonia, and compost temperature is further reduced to 24°C by introduction of fresh air, if there is no smell of ammonia it is ready for the spawning,

**Bulk Pasteurization or Tunnel Pasteurization**

In this process, the compost is treated in bulk inside a specially built room known as the tunnel. The compost is filled in the bulk chamber upto the height of 2-2.2 m, in such a way that one square meter of space occupies approximately 900-1000 kg of compost. Several temperature sensors are placed at different points of the tunnel to measure the temperature. One sensor is placed below the plenum in the ventilation duct below the grated floor, two or three are placed inside the compost mass and two above the compost for air temperature. Immediately after filling, all the doors are closed and blower is switched on to bring down the compost at uniform temperature of 45 °C. When the compost temperature reaches 45°C, introduction of fresh air is stopped. Compost temperature starts rising @ 1-2°C/h. Required temperature (57-58°C) needed for pasteurization of compost may reach in 10-12 h. Some quantity of steam can also be used for the purpose. This process is called pasteurization or kill. It will eliminate harmful insects, nematodes and competitor moulds from the compost and at the same time will preserve the nutrients in the compost which can effectively be utilized by *A. bisporus* mycelium.

After kill the temperature is usually maintained till there is no detectable smell of ammonia (less than 10 ppm) in the compost. This phase is known as conditioning of the compost which is normally accomplished in 3-4 days. After conditioning, the temperature of the compost is further gradually brought down to 25-30°C by introduction of fresh air in the tunnel and when this temperature reaches the compost, it is ready for spawning.

## Advantages of bulk pasteurization

1. More compost per unit size of the room can be treated as compared to tray pasteurization.
2. The cost of pasteurization in tunnel is less than tray system.
3. Wooden trays which are very costly now-a-days are not required in this process.
4. Same tunnel can be utilized for spawn run in bulk which gives effective use of the space.
5. Yield per unit weight of compost is generally higher than the tray pasteurization.

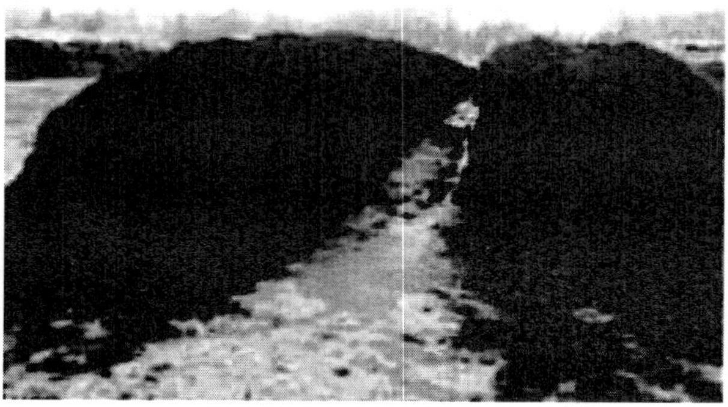

**Compost pile**

### c. Indoor composting

Compost prepared either by LMC or SMC involves traditional outdoor composting which causes environmental problems. Large amount of malodorous gases viz., ammonia, methane, hydrogen sulfide and other methylated sulphur compounds are emitted in the atmosphere creating nuisance among the masses. This foul smell is generally emitted when the compost is fermented at high temperature under anaerobic conditions. In Netherlands, Australia and other European countries, rules governing law of pollution (emission of odour) have become very stringent resulting in closer of many composting units where short method of composting is involved. Need is therefore felt to control the composting process in such a manner, so there is least possibility of environmental pollution and at the same time to monitor the whole composting procedure specially aeration and temperature in such a fashion resulting in an end product most suitable for the growth of mushroom mycelium in the shortest possible time (Harper *et al.,* 1992). In the light of above facts work on production of such substrate started way back in 1967 at France where whole composting process is carried out indoors in specially built tunnels and hence the name indoor composting (Laborde, 1992). Since such compost is produced under total environmental controlled conditions, sometimes it is also called environmentally controlled composting (ECC) (Gulliver *et al.,* 1991) or rapid indoor composting (REC), or aerated rapid composting (ARC) (Laborde, 1993).

Due to the environmental legislations phase - I of composting is being performed indoor in Netherlands from 1995 onwards (Straatsma *et al.,* 1995a). Indoor composting method which is bulk process where phase I is carried out in indoors at around 80°C for 2-3 days and then phase II at 50°C for 5-7 days except for a short peak heat at 58"C.

## 2. Filling of Tray Beds

Prepared compost is spread on the platform and 3 kg of calcium carbonate is added. Compost is filled in all corners and edges of a tray and compressed fairly in the tray using a wooden board leaving 1 cm clear space on the top of the tray.

**Cropping of button mushroom**

3. **Spawning**

Spawning means planting mushroom mycelium and growing on a suitable substrate, in the compost. Spawning methods *viz.*, surface spawning, layer spawning, thorough spawning, spot spawning, active mycelium spawning and shake up spawning are followed. *A. bisporus* spawn is especially grown on wheat or sorghum grains in specialized spawn laboratories. It is prepared and sold in India by several *Go*vernment and non-government agencies. One such Central Government Institute is the National Centre for Mushroom Research and Training (NCMRT), Chambaghat, Solan 173213 (HP), India.

Spawning is done by spreading the spawn on tray beds when half filled with compost and again after the tray is filled completely. During spawning, the spawn is gently mixed with fore-fingers and pressed uniformly each time. The trays are covered with newspaper sheets and sprinkled with water to provide humidity. The inoculated trays are stacked vertically, one over the other, depending on the height of the room. Water spraying is continued twice a day or less depending upon available humidity in the atmosphere through the spawn running and cropping period.

## 4. Temperature maintenance

Temperature of the room is maintained between 24 and 25°C for 12-15 days for running of the spawn, i.e. formation of mycelium strands all over the tray beds. White cottony mycelium over the compost surface and colour of the compost that changes from dark to light brown which is indicative of successful completion of spawn running period.

**Harvesting stage of button mushroom**

## 5. Casing

Casing means covering the compost with a thin layer of soil or soil like material after the spawn has spread in the compost **(spawn run).** Soil has been the universal casing material. But all soils as such cannot be used as 'casing soil' with advantage, so it is especially prepared soil that can be used for casing. In India, a number of mixtures have been recommended: (a) well rotten cow dung, mixed with light soil in 3:1 ratio; (b) soil and sand in the ratio of 1:1, (c) farm yard manure and gravel, ratio 4:1; (d) farm yard manure and loam ratio 1:1; (e) soil peat mixture 2:1, and spent compost, sand and slaked lime (4:1:1) and nematicide mixture. Of these, the last combination is most often used.

**Preparation of casing soil**

Four parts of spent compost with one part of sand are mixed to which 5 kg of slaked lime per cubic metre of compost is added. The mixture is treated with a nematicide, by spraying or sprinkling it at the rate of 5 ml per cm. The material in a pile (1.2 m x 1.0m) is left under a tree shade for a period of one year, turning it every 4 months. Spent compost is sieved, which turns into black soil in one year, for removal of under composted lumps. Casing soil is observed for black colour and pH. A pH between 8.0 and 8.5 is the most suitable for mushroom yield. pH of the casing soil is adjusted, if desired, by the addition of lime or carbonate of lime or free stone to the casing mixture.

**Sterilization of casing soil**

The casing material is sterilized either by the chemicals (formalin, chloropicrin, methyl bromide or vapam) or by heating or by steam from boiler through perforated pipes and temperature raised to 70-75°C and maintained for 6 hours. The purpose of sterilization is to kill harmful microorganisms (fungi, nematodes, insects).

**Casing the beds**

The newspaper sheets are removed from the spawned beds after 3 weeks and the compost is gently pressed with the help of wooden board. Then the beds are covered with 2-2.5 cm thick layer of sterilized casing material.

**6. Watering of beds**

Water is sprayed over the beds with a fine nozzle of a sprayer to maintain relative humidity between 70 and 80 per cent.

**Observations** : Mushroom beds are observed for crop which can be expected 5 to 20 days after casing. Mushrooms mostly appear in *"flushes"* and at a temperature of 15°C, it generally takes 7 to 8 days to come to the button stage from the first appearance of the formation of a pin-head. There is an interval of 8 to 10 days between flushes.

## 7. Harvesting of mushrooms

Harvesting should be done everyday (in the morning and evening. depending upon the market demand) to get a good quality of mushrooms (the cap still being tight to its stalk is the right stage to harvest the mushrooms).

Harvesting is done by holding the cap with fore-fingers slightly pressed against the soil and twisted out. The mycelial strands and soil particles clinging to the base of the stalk (stem) are cut off with a knife. Specially designed wooden box is used for collection of mushrooms from multistoried trays, each provided with the hooks for resting it against the side board of the mushroom tray.

## 8. Storage

Mushrooms are stored at 4°C in a refrigerator for a few days to avoid the quality deterioration, because mushrooms are a highly perishable commodity. The white colour turns brown and then black in a couple of hours at high summer temperature. Soon after water oozes out and the mushrooms become unfit for cooking,

### Precautions

1. Always prepare compost with wheat-straw over 300 kg in quantity, as the heat generated in smaller piles will not be sufficient for fermentation.
2. The compost pile should not become hard pressed to avoid anaerobic conditions as decomposition takes place only under aerobic conditions.

3. If ammonia smell is noticeable, more turnings of the compost should be done to free the compost from ammonia smell.
4. Care should be taken to wet the composting material to the extent that water drops do not ooze out, if the compost is squeezed in the palm of hand.
5. Water should never be poured over the spawn to avoid the failure of the crop.
6. Proper care should be taken not to allow the temperature to rise above 75°C so that useful microorganisms present in the soil are not killed. Care should be taken to leave at least one metre clear space in between the last tray and the ceiling, so that air circulation is not impaired.

**Button mushroom trays**

# UNIT - 8
# CULTIVATION OF PADDY STRAW MUSHROOM

Genus *Volvariella* belongs to family Volvaceae of order Agaricales. It is one of the most important genera and a large number of species have been described from all over the world. There are 12 species of *Volvariella re*corded from India. Six species are important and are found in different parts of India, *viz., V. bombycina, V. diplasia, V. esculenta, V. speciosa, V. terrestrius* and V. *volvaceae.*

*V. volvaceae* and V. *diplasia* are commonly known as paddy straw mushroom. They are widely cultivated in China, Thailand and Phillipines. In India, it was brought to cultivation in 1943 in Madras but commercial cultivation is yet to become popular in our country. Because of low efficiency (20-30%), our farmers are not ready to take up paddy straw mushroom cultivation.

**Substrate preparation**

This mushroom grows best in paddy straw but several other straws can also be used for its cultivation. Recently composted coir and cotton waste have given good results. Old contaminated and rotten paddy straw is not suitable for its cultivation. The straw is tied into bundles of 1.2 m long and 25 cm diameter in size. These bundles are steeped in water in cemented tank for 18-24 hrs. The bundles are taken out and put on a cemented ground for few hrs for draining out the excess water.

**Bed preparation and spawning**

Mushroom beds are prepared on a raised bamboo platform inside a thatched hut. Four pre-wet bundles are placed side by side on this platform facing all the loose ends on one side.

Another four bundles are placed with their loose ends on the opposite sides. The loose ends of all 8 bundles meet and overlap each other in the middle. Spawn is applied on this first layer about 15 cm away from the outer layer edge. On the top of spawned first layer, a little quantity of sterilized red grain powder (about 200 g/bed) is applied along with spawn. On top of spawned first layer of 8 bundles, again a second layer of 8 bundles is placed at right angles of previous layer are in a criss-cross fashion. It is also spawned in the same way. Third layer is again laid on top of the second layer in a criss-cross fashion and spawned. Final layer of 8 bundles is placed on the third layer. This layer is spawned and covered with a thin layer of loose straw. Finally bed is gently pressed down to make it compact for effective spawn and to avoid rapid water loss, it is covered with polythene sheets or gunny sheets. For preparing one mushroom bed, 350-400 g grain spawn is required.

**Paddy straw mushroom**

### Spawn running

Individual beds are watered daily with a rose cane once or twice depending upon climatic condition. Total dry weight of straw is 25-30 kg/bed, A minimum of 18-20 litres of water/bed is sprayed to maintain moisture level of 65-70%. It takes 10-15 days to complete the mycelial growth under optimum condition of 30-35°C temperature with 85-90%RH.

### Mushroom production

Spawn run beds are exposed to fresh air and mushroom start appearing within a few days. These are picked at button stage early in the morning. Fruiting bodies are separated from adhering straw. Mushroom production continues for 2-4 weeks. Each bed of 30 kg dry straw can produce 4-6 kg of fresh mushroom. It can be cultivated in North Indian plains from May to September and in peninsular India from March to November. When mushroom production stops, straw can be composted to manure. This is very tasty and valued for its excellent aroma.

**Paddy straw mushroom**

# UNIT - 9
# OTHER CULTIVABLE MUSHROOMS

## 1) Shiitake mushroom

*Lentinus edodes (Lentinellus edodes*) is called as shiitake mushroom in Japan, where it is cultivated. It has been in cultivation in Japan and China from very olden days since 2000 years. This is a lignicolous fungus, which may grow up **on wood** logs. It is normally grown using logs from some important trees grown using logs from some important tree species like shii, chestnut and oak. Logs of oak (*Quercus serrata and Q. acutissima*) are very commonly used. However, in recent years cultivation of this mushroom on artificially prepared substrates is being red in several countries. Generally substrates prepared by mixing sawdust, bran etc., are known to support the growth.

**Shiitake mushroom**

### Plastic bag method

In Taiwan, a new substrate base has been prepared for successful cultivation of this mushroom under artificial conditions. The substrate used in the new process is a mixture of saw dust of a broad leaved tree (90 %), rice bran (10 %) and calcium carbonate (0.2%) with 65 % moisture. The moistened mixture is placed in plastic bags (16.5 x 33.5 cm) and sterilized at 121° C for 1 hr. After 2-3 months of incubation, the plastic bags are opened for fruiting under 16-22° C and Relative Humidity of 90-95 %.

### 2. Wood ear or Jew's ear mushroom

The fruiting bodies look like the human ear and hence they are called as wood ear and Jew's ear mushroom. The important species are *Auricularia auricula (A. auricula – judae*) and *A. polytricha.*

This is one of the earliest known edible mushrooms in China and has been in cultivation for nearly 2000 years. At present it is extensively cultivated in Taiwan. Commonly the logs of trees like *Morus australis, Rhus verniciflura, Magnolia obovata, Acacia confusa, Ficus retusa, F. stipulosa, Pongamia pinnata, Gardonia jasminodes* and *Bombax ceiba* etc., are used for cultivation. However, in recent years Polybag technique has been developed in Taiwan. Small huts are constructed using bamboo and straw for cultivation.

### Poly bag method

Saw dust is mixed thoroughly with 20 % bran and a little of calcium carbonate to adjust the pH. This mixture is taken in a polybag of special quality of about 15-20 cm length and 10-20 cm in diameter and sterilized at 90-100 °C for 90 minutes. After cooling they are inoculated and incubated in the mushroom house at 25 -28°C. After spawn run, both the ends of bag are cut open and arranged in bamboo frames for buttoning. The yield per bag ranges from 50-500 g.

### 3. Winter mushroom

The sporospores of mushroom normally appear in winter and hence the name. *Flammulina velutipes* is the mushroom collected wildly from forest areas and consumed in ancient Japan. At present, it is cultivated mainly in Japan and Taiwan. Cultivation was started on wood logs as in other wood destroying mushrooms. However, in recent years they are cultivated using saw dust-bran mixture.

*Flammulina mushroom*

**Procedure**

Sawdust and bran are well mixed at 4:1 ratio and filled in Polypropylene bottles and capped. They are sterilized at 100°C for 1 h. After cooling, the bottles were inoulated with spawn and incubated for spawn run. Optimun ternperature for spawn run is 22-26°C and for fruiting body formation is 10-12° C. After spawn run the caps are removed and bottles are incubated in dark at a temperature of 10-12°C and relative humidity of 80-85 %. In another 10 15 days primordia are formed and at that time the temperature has to be lowered to 3-5°C. The mushrooms are harvested when the stipe length is 13-14 cm and bundled. The yield may be 150-250 g per bottle. It takes about 50-60 days from initial fruiting to cropping. The same bottle can be used for a second crop, which may about 100-150 g/ bottle.

## 4. Garden giant mushroom

This mushroom, *Stropharia ruggosannulata,* was first cultivated in Germany. The mushroom has a very wide sporocarp, usually upto 40 cm in diameter The colour of the mushroom is yellow or brown with a red tint. Usually straw is used as substrate.

### Procedure

Fresh straw is cut into small pieces and soaked in water for 48hr. The wet straw is piled on the ground at a height of about 25 cm, in one sq. m. area. Spawn in inoculated at 500 g per pile. Small pieces of spawn are placed to a depth of 5-8 cm and it is slightly pressed down. Spawn run is usually good at 20-30° C. The beds are kept covered with sacks or sheets of newspapers and compressed with weighted boards. When the surface growth appears, the cover is removed and a thin layer of moist humid soil is spread over the bed. In another 30-40 days time first harvest can be done, and it will continue for about 2- 3 months. An average yield of 600 g/kg of dry straw will be obtained.

## 5. Nameko mushroom

*Pholiota nameko* is commonly called as nameko mushroom, which is widely cultivated in Japan. Under natural conditions, the mushroom grows on the woods of many trees. The wild species of *Quercus* is the most common substrate. The pileus of the mushroom is yellowish brown and is covered by a gelatinous mucilage and hence the name in Japan.

**Procedure**

The sawdust from the selected trees is stored for about a year and then mixed with bran and wetted properly. The mixture is filled in special type of polypropylene bottles and steam sterilized. After cooling the bottles are inoculated with spawn to get the mushroom.

**6. Silver ear mushroom:**

This mushroom, *Tremella fuciformisis* also called as white jelly fungus grows naturally on dead tree trunks in China. The fruit bodies have a number of lobes on which the hymenium is found. The margin of the pileus is lobed and curved. They occur in clusters of about 10 cm in width. They vary in colour from transparent opaque, white grey. The old techniques of cultivation was very primitive wherein the infected wood logs are collected and stacked along with the suitable logs for natural infection and fruiting. In recent years, special type of logs is inoculated with spawn prepared in saw dust–bran mixture. The logs of trees like *Rhus succdanea, Fagus* spp. *Eugenia jambosa* and *Mangifera indica* are used. Small holes made in the wood logs at regular intervals and are spawned, closed and covered with plastic sheets. The mushroom can be harvested after two months after spawning and harvesting can be continued for about 7 more months.

# UNIT - 10
# PESTS, DISEASES AND WEED MOULDS OF MUSHROOMS

## Pests of mushrooms

### a. Sciarid flies

*Bradysia paupera, B.tritici; Lycorella avripila* The larvae restricts the spawn run and form tunnels from the root portion towards the cap. The infected buttons turned brown and leathery and ultimately rots.

Adult *B. tritici* is greyish black in colour. The abdomen of male fly terminates in claspers and in female, the abdomen is swollen with ovipositor.

Larvae: Shining black head. Fully grown larvae is dirty white with visible longitudinal black streaks.

#### Management

1. Strict hygiene and sanitation are the primary method of pest control.
2. Fixing screens on doors and ventilators with nylon net of 35 or >35 mesh effectively check the entry of flies in the cropping room.
3. Malathion 0.05% spray on infested areas.

### b. Phorids : *Megaselia sandhui, M.tamilnadulensis*

The larvae feeds gregariously and form tunnels. The attacked mushroom turns brown. Attack at pinning stage restricts the further developinent of buttons.

Adult: Hump backed, light to dark brown

Larvae: Dirty white with visible blackish "mouth hooks"

**Phorid flies**

## Management

1. Strict hygiene and sanitation are the primary method of pest control.
2. Fixing screens on doors and ventilators with nylon net of 35 or >35 mesh effectively check the entry of flies in the cropping room.
3. Malathion 0.05% spray on infested areas.

**c. Spring tails :** *Seria iricolor, Lepidocyrtus cyancus*

Adult: Ground colour with light violet coloured band along the side of the body without forming a definite pattern.

Adults and nymphs feed on mycelium and thus arrest spawn run. They produce shallow pits on sporophore.

## Management

1. Strict hygiene
2. Efficient pasteurization of compost
3. Malathion 0.05% spray on infested areas.

**Spring tails**

**Mites**

*Tyrogyphus putrescentiae, Histiostoma beinemanni, Hypoaspis mali*

They differ with the species of mites. Cavities, deep pits, tunnels or holes are seen on the mushroom. Mites attack the mycelium and restricts its growth.

**Management**

1. Proper hygiene, sanitation and pasteurization of compost and casing material.
2. Spray dicofol 0.1% in mushroom house.
3. Sterilization of trays.

On any account, spraying of insecticide should not be done over mushroom beds.

**Nematodes**

*Ditylenchus myceliophagus, Aphelenchoides composticola*

Nematodes secrete strong cellulose invertase and chitinase and convert the mushroom into assimilable forms. Some of the typical symptoms produced by nematode attack are mycelial growth sparse, patchy and tums stingy, white spawn run slowly turns brown, sporophore flush poor and delayed, violet colour gills.

## Management

1. Strict hygiene and sanitation and proper pasteurization of compost.
2. Composting yard, wall, floors etc should be disinfested with 4% fomalin.
3. Covering the compost with double PVC sheet for 24hrs after 3rd turning gives effective control.

## Diseases of mushrooms

## Fungal Diseases

a. **Dry bubble/*V*erticillium diseases/Brown spot, Fungus spot or La mole:**
   ***Verticillium fungicola* var *fungicola***

## Symptoms

Whitish mycelial growth is initially noticed on the casing soil which tums greyish yellow. Infection at pinning stage results in typical onion shaped mushroom. At later stages, it is crooked and deformed. On one side of the stipe, restricted growth occurs and on the other side normal growth occurs, hence surface tissues peel away from the curved side. Harelip symptoms occurs when the part of the cap is affected. Appearance of the brown spots on cap which later turn grey are the typical symptoms. In severe cases, mouldy fuzz on mushroom is noticed.

## Management

1. Strict hygiene should be maintained during cultivation of mushroom
2. Common salt is used to minimize the spread.
3. Spray with Dithane Z 78 (0.02 - 0.05%) or topsin, or chlorothalonil have been found effective with 2% commercial formalin. Infected patches should be removed and disposed properly by burying or burning.

**b. Wet bubble : *Mycogone periciosa***

**Symptoms**

The mushroom tissues become distorted, disfigured and form a brown sclerodermoid mass which are initially white and fluffy but later becomes brown. In the case of very high humidity, amber to dark brown drops of liquid develops on the surface of the undifferentiated tissues. The affected gill exhibits an myceiial growth.

**Management**

1. Use of sterilized casing soil and proper hygiene avoids infection.
2. Use of zineb or maneb or chlorothalonil or thiabendozole.

**c. Cob web disease *: Cladobotryum dendroides***

**Symptoms**

On the surface of the casing small, circular white patch of the mycelium is noticed. As the disease progresses a fluffy white mould grows over the mushrooms, ultimately it turns brown, rots and die off. The white colour of the mycelium turns pink or red with age.

**Management**

The casing soil is thoroughly disinfected with live steam (50°C for 4 h) formaldehyde or treated with benomyl 150 g/110 $m^2$ upon casing.

Temperature and RH during picking should not go beyond 19°C and 90% respectively, as they favour the development of the disease.

**Bacterial Diseases**

**a. Brown blotch: *Pseudomonas tolasii***

**Symptoms**

Yellow to light brown spots are produced initially on the surface of the mushroom caps, later brown sunken spots of variable size develops and are greasy to touch. High humidity, low temperature and surface films of water on mushroom caps favour the development of infection.

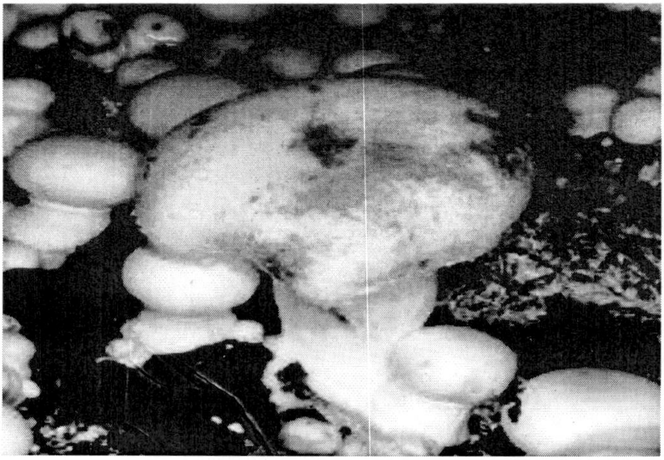

**Brown blotch disease**

**Management**

Proper sterilization of casing soil, sanitation, reducing the humidity in the room by minimizing the number of water spray and improved aeration so as to introduce sufficient fresh air inside the cropping room and spray of chlorinated water (100-150 ppm) at 3 or 4 days interval checks infection.

Biological control agents like *Pseudomonas fluorescens* are added immediately after pasteurization to prevent the build up of the pathogen.

**Virus diseases**

a. La France disease
b. Die-back disease
c. Brown disease
d. Watery stipe
e. X-disease.

The following general symptoms are produced by viral infection.

1. Mycelium does not permeate or hardly permeates the casing layer or disappears after normal spread.
2. A delay in appearance of pin head.
3. Sporophore appears below the casing rather than on the casing surface.
4. Early opening or off white colour cap.
5. Forms a drum stick type of fruit body.
6. Elongated, thin and slightly bent stipe or thickened barrel shaped stipe or spongy brown stipe.
7. Water soaked lesion on top of the stipe and the mushroom: topples down by slight touch.
8. Veil is absent or abnormal, hard gills develop.
9. Musty, small, mushroom becomes shriveled, leathery and brown.

**Physiological disorder**

As compared to white button mushroom, there are few physiological disorders recorded in oyster mushrooms. Reduced light in the cropping room results in longer and thicker stipes and pileus is partly reduced. Insufficient ventilation (1-2% carbon dioxide) and low light exposure induce bunched growth regeneration.

**Weed moulds of oyster mushrooms**

**Weed moulds in beds**

Normally the beds are contaminated either before or after opening with moulds like i) Green moulds- *Aspergillus, Penicillium, Trichoderma*. ii) Olive green mould-*Chaetomium* sp iii) Inky caps *Coprinus* sp iv) *Sclerotium sp, Rhizopus* sp and M*ucor* species are observed in the substrate.

**Weed moulds (contaminants) in spawn**

*Aspergillus, Penicillium, Trichoderma* and *Rhizopus* species are the weed moulds affect the spawn growth

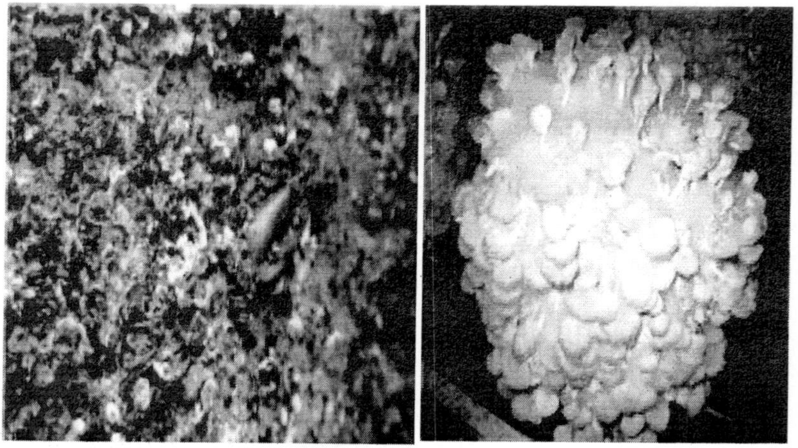

**Weed moulds**

**Precautions to avoid weed moulds in spawn**

1. Always prepare the spawn in a clean room.
2. Avoid room with high temperature
3. Dusty rooms and use of unsterilized materials should be avoided.
4. Ensure proper cooking and correct proportion of mixing of $CaCO_3$, to encourage good growth of spawn.
5. Introduce sufficient inoculum into spawn bottle.
6. Avoid loose plucking of spawn bottles.
7. Maintain sterile condition in culture room
   - Avoid frequent opening of culture room.
   - Always keep the room, free of dust and micro organisms by swabbing all surfaces exposed to air with 1% Dettol or any other antiseptic solution.
   - Switch on UV lamp for 20-30 minutes before using the room.
   - Once in a month or once in 2 months fumigate the culture room; for this take, 10 g of $KMnO_4$ in a beaker and add 20 ml of formalin. Keep the beaker in culture room; (for a room of 1.5x1.5x2.2 m) and close the door. Fumes generated will circulate inside the room and kill the microorganisms. Keep the room closed

for 24 hrs. Use the room after 24-36 hrs to avoid irritation to eyes.

8. Make adequate precautions during inoculation in culture room.
   - Close the door quickly after entering the room.
   - Always keep the door closed.
   - Do not indulge in dialogue when inside.
   - Carefully open the spawn bag or test tube by keeping very near the flame and quickly heat the mouth of bottle or test tube.
   - All the materials and accessories used for inoculation should be sterile (should be heated well over the flame)
   - Quick transfer the inoculum.
   - Ensure the proper sterilization of spawn bottle.

**Precautions to avoid competitors in mushroom beds**

1. Select good quality spawn for mushroom bed preparation
2. Boil the straw properly as described earlier.
3. Do not use the water used for soaking the straw for boiling.
4. Always use the fresh water for boiling straw.
5. Always prepare beds indoor, use disinfected gunny cloth and room
6. Maintain optimum moisture straw
7. Relative humidity should be regulated as desired.
8. If mould growth is noticed in small patches on the beds, carefully cut out the affected area and swab the area with 0.05% carbendazim or 0.1% Mancozeb. Burn the removed patch of mould carefully. .
9. Dispose the contaminated beds by deeply, burying then, in a distant place/by carefully burning them. This avoids further spread of moulds.
10. In the case of frequent contamination in beds, keep either in spawn running/cropping room remove all the beds and fumigate the room by spraying 6 ml of dichlorvas + 200 ml of formalin in 10 litre of water. Close the doors and ventilators for 24 hrs and use the room after 24 - 48 hrs.

# UNIT - 11
# MEDICINAL AND NUTRITIONAL VALUE OF MUSHROOMS

The medicines of mushroom origin have got an ancient history. The religious scriptures like "vedas have mentioned its medicinal values. The Greeks regarded mushroom as "Providing strength to soldiers in war" and the Romans considered as "Foods of Gods and the Chinese treated them as Élixir of life. Chang and Buswell (1966) have coined the term Mushroom nutriceuticals for the medicinal preparation from mushrooms.

Mushrooms are valuable health food - low in calories, high in vegetable proteins, chitin, iron, zinc, fiber, essential amino acids, vitamins and minerals. Mushrooms also have a long history of use in Traditional Chinese Medicine. Their legendary effects on promoting good health and vitality and increasing our body's adaptive abilities have been supported by recent studies. These studies suggest that mushrooms are probiotic they help our body strengthen itself and fight off illness by maintaining physiological homeostasis-restoring our body's balance and natural resistance to disease. The compounds they contain have been classified as Host Defense Potentiators (HDP) which can have immune system enhancement properties. That is one of the reasons they are currently used as adjuncts to cancer treatments in Japan and China. In Japan, Russia, China, and the U.S.A. several different polysaccharide anti tumor agents have been developed from the fruiting body, mycelia, and culture medium of various medicinal mushrooms *(Lentinus edodes, Ganoderma lucidum, Schizophyllum commune, Trametes versicolor, Inonotus obliquus, and Flammulina velutipes*). Both cellular components and secondary metabolites of a large number of mushrooms have been shown to effect the immune system of the host and therefore could be used to treat a variety of disease states.

Many scientific studies performed in universities and medical facilities have produced volumes of studies on the medicinal effects of mushrooms on many different ailments affecting humans. For example: *Reishi* has been called an "immune potentiator" and can increase the production of Interleukin-1and 2 and "exerted an inhibition effect on tumor growth and other effects: Analgesic, Anti-inflammatory, Antioxidant, Antiviral through inducing interferon production, Lowers blood pressure, Cardiotonic action through lowering serum cholesterol, Expectorant and Antitussive, liver (Hepatitis) protecting and detoxifying protection against ionizing radiation, Antibacterial, and Anti HIV activity. Reishi contains calcium, iron and phosphorus as well as vitamins C, D, and B including pantothenic acid, which is essential to nerve function and the adrenal glands. An extract (Lentinan) from *Shiitake (*for centuries called "Elixir of Life") has been licensed as a anti-cancer drug by the Japanese FDA. Lentinan has shown some effects on bowel cancer, liver cancer, stomach cancer, ovarian cancer and lung cancer.

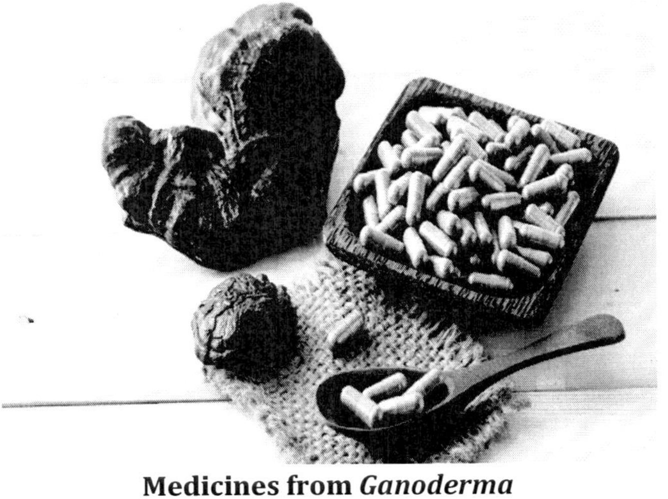

**Medicines from *Ganoderma***

One of the species of *Cordyceps* can be a powerful stimulant for macrophage activity, strengthening your immune systein's ability to fight against bacterial and viral infection. Human clinical studies indicate that *Cordyceps* can be effective for treatment of high cholesterol, poor libido/ impotence, arrhythmia, lung cancer, and chronic kidney failure. It is also reported that *Cordyceps* causes smooth muscle relaxation and helpful for treating chronic coughs, asthma, and other bronchial conditions. Recent human clinical studies have indicated that *Tremella fuciformis (*Bai Mu Erh) stimulates the immune system, demonstrates anti-tumor activity, lowers LDL cholesterol, protects the liver and is anti-inflammatory and may slow the aging process. ***Grifola frondosa*** (Maitake) has also been shown to stimulate the immune system and to be effective against some tumors.

**Medicinal mushroom – *Lentinus edodes***

Many of the compounds found in Shiitake, Reishi, *Cordyceps,* and some other mushrooms are classified as Host Defense Potentiators (HDP). These compounds include: hemicellulose polysaccharides, polysaccharide-peptides, nucleosides, triterpeniods complex starches, and other metabolitcs. It is believed that combinations of these products target the human immune system as well as aid in neuron transmission, metabolism, hormonal balance and the transport of nutrients and oxygen. Through a host-mediated (T cell) immune mechanism, they help the body to regulate the development of lymphoid stem cells and other important defense responses.

## Medicines from poisonous mushrooms

1. The poisonous mushrooms in China have been considered "as using of poison as a antidote for poison".
2. *Amanita muscaria* (fly agaric) used therapeutically as a powder, tincture for swollen glands, nervous troubles, epilepsy, ailment of heart, inflammation of eyes, etc.,
3. Homoeopathic medicines under the name "agar", "agaris" or "agarus" are available.
4. Muscinol and ibotenic acid, the 2 compounds prepared from *A. muscaria* can cure as schizophorenia characterized by the malfunctioning of the GABA (Gama Amino Butryic Acid).
5. Psilocybin and psilosin extracted from *Psilocybe mericana* used to treat mental disorders.
6. *Amanita phaloides* extracts are used against cholera and intermittent fever.
7. Ganodermin is produced from *Ganoderma* sp is used to resist the diseases and to improve the health.

**Table 4 Medicines from edible mushrooms**

| S. No. | Mushroom | Medicinal value |
|---|---|---|
| 1 | *Agaricus bisporus* | Stimulating digestion, curing hypertension. |
| 2 | *Auricularia polytrichar* | Strengthening health, helping blood circulation, piles, stomach ailment. |
| 3 | *Boletus edulis* | Cure muscles and joints to relax |
| 4 | *Coriolus versicolor* | Curing chronic diseases |
| 5 | *Ganoderma lucidum* (Mushroom of immortality - Japan "Longevity mushroom-Korea) | Rejuvenating effect, relieve stress, increase working efficiency, neurasthenia, curing hypertension, Antiviral effects, Anti HIV, anti Hepatitis B, Epstein Barrvirus and antitumour activity. |
| 6 | *Grifola frondosa* | Strengthening health and resisting disease, anti-tumour activity. |
| 7 | *Hericium erinaceus* | Beneficial to heart, kidneys, liver, spleen, gastric ulcers. |
| 8 | *Lentinus edodes* | Strengthening health and resisting disease, blood pressure, hyperacidity, anti-tumour effect, anti-cancerous and anti-virus. |
| 9 | *Pleurotus ostreatus* | Cause muscles and joints to relax. |
| 10 | *Tremella fuciformis* | Strengthening health and resisting disease |
| 11 | *Tricholoma mongolicum* | Beneficial to stomach and intestines. |
| 12 | *Volvariella volvaceae* | Cures blood pressure. |

The Ajino-Moto Company of Japan has suggested that the Lentinan sulphate of shitake could inhibit the development of AIDS virus and based on this the Food and Drugs Administration of USA have recently approved the use of shitake extract for clinical trials against AIDS. *Ganoderma* spores are marketed as Lingzhi in Singapore which is used for resisting disease and strengthening health. Very learned and well experienced Ayurvedic practitioners of Kerala give "Nilamanga preparations for various ailments. Nilamanga is mango shaped and is usually associated with old termite nests. Boiled extract with gingelly oil is applied internally to cure ear pain in children. Crushed Nilamanga in butter mixture if applied externally will cure body abscissions. Boiled milk extracts of this mushroom is said to be an incomparable oral medicine for treating jaundice.

## Nutritional value of Mushrooms

Mushroom with their flavour, texture, nutritional value, very high productivity per unit area and time, less dependence on land and ability to grow on a variety of residual agricultural wastes, have rightly been recognized by FAO as food contributing to the protein nutrition of the countries.

**Shiitake mushroom**

## Nutritive value of fresh mushrooms

Cereals, the staple constituents of Indian diet are deficient in two essential amino acids, namely lysine and tryptophan. Mushrooms which are rich in lysine and tryptophan can effectively supplement the cereals in terms of proteins.

**Table 5 Essential amino acids (% crude protein) in edible mushrooms**

| *Aminoacid* | *A.bisporus* | *P. Sajor caju* | *V. volvaceae* |
|---|---|---|---|
| Leucine | 7.5 | 7.0 | 4.5 |
| Isoleucine | 4.5 | 4.4 | 3.4 |
| Valine | 2.5 | 5.3 | 5.4 |
| Tryptophan | 2.0 | 1.2 | 1.5 |
| Lysine | 9.1 | 5.7 | 7.1 |
| Threonme | 5.5 | 5.0 | 3.5 |
| Phenyl alanine | 4.2 | 5.0 | 2.6 |
| Methonine | 0.9 | 1.8 | 1.1 |
| Histidine | 2.7 | 2.2 | 3.8 |

***Tremella fuciformis***

Like most vegetables, mushrooms are rich in minerals and vitamins.

**Table 6 Vitamins and minerals in mushrooms**

| Vitamins / Minerals | Mg/100 g of fresh mushroom | |
|---|---|---|
| | *Pleurotus sp* | *Volvariella volvaceae* |
| Vitamins | | |
| Thiamine | 0.5 | 0.14 |
| Riboflavin | 0.5 | 0.61 |
| Niacin | 10.9 | 2.40 |
| Minerals | | |
| Ca | 3.3 | 5.60 |
| P | 134.8 | 100.0 |
| Fe | 1.5 | 1.7 |
| Na | 83.7 | 80.00 |
| K | 379.3 | 325.00 |

It is also important to realize that mushrooms contain vitamins not occurring in green plants such as B1, B2, B6, B12, D1, D2 and pantothenic acids. Their low sugar, low calorie and high fibrous nature are the added advantage.

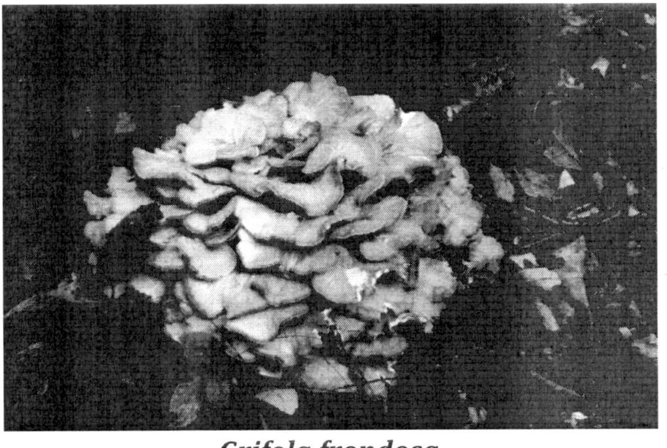

***Grifola frondosa***

# UNIT - 12
# PRESERVATION OF MUSHROOMS

The mushrooms can be preserved by canning or dehydration. The canned mushroom can be used for preparation in recipes after draining the brine solution. The dehydrated product is to be rehydrated in boiling water before use.

**Canning of mushrooms**

Fresh mushroom are highly perishable in nature and can not be stored for more than 24 hours at room temperature or one to two weeks at low temperature (0°C) without suffering a loss in quality. Mushrooms can however be processed into various products like canned mushrooms, dehydrated mushrooms, mushroom soups, mushroom ketchup, mushroom pickle etc.

Canning of mushrooms as contrasted to other products forms an important outlet for processing. Mushrooms are canned in brine, butter or cream which are used in recipes for a great variety of products.

**Canned mushroom**

1. **Harvesting of mushrooms:** Mushrooms are harvested at the round stage when they come out of the soil as small buttons. Each button is cut neatly with a sharp blade with 0.5 to 1.0 cm long stalk attached to the cap.
2. **Washing of mushrooms:** The buttons are trimmed and washed gently in water to remove any adhering soil.
3. **Blanching of mushrooms:** Later the mushrooms are dipped in boiling water for 2-3 minutes and put in cold water. To prevent leaching losses in water, which are sometimes as high as 25%, the blanching can also be done in steam for the same time.
4. **Filling into sanitary cans:** Blanched and cooled mushroom are filled into the can to about 1.25 cm of its height. Approximately 195 g mushrooms are filled in 1 lb jam can.
5. **Addition of salt solution:** Salt solution containing 2% common salt, 2% sugar and 0.3% citric acid is prepared, filtered through a piece of cloth and added boiling hot to the can to fill just upto the brim (125 ml solution for 1 lb jam can)
6. **Exhausting the cans:** After putting the lid on the can, the cans are kept in boiling water or steam till their centre reaches a temperature of 80-85$^0$C.
7. **Sealing of cans:** Cans are sealed on a steamer to get an air tight seal.
8. **Sterilization of cans**: The one lb jam size cans are later steamed in a pressure cooker at 115°C (10 lb/sq inch) for 25 minutes. This time should be increased or decreased depending upon the larger or the smaller size of the can.
9. **Cooling of cans**: Soon after sterilization, the cans are kept in cold water for cooling.
10. **Storage of cans**: Cans are wiped dry and kept in a cool dry place.

### Dehydration of mushrooms

Mushrooms for dehydration, unlike for canning are harvested at a mature stage. Their muddy stalk ends are trimmed and if these are too big they are cut into small pieces.

Mushrooms can be dried in the sun or in a mechanical dehydrator at 60-70°C. Although majority of mushrooms are sun dried, yet the related and advantages of quicker drying in a dust-free atmosphere in a mechanical drier are obvious. After complete drying, the mushrooms are reduced about 1/8$^{th}$-1/12$^{th}$ of their weight depending upon the variety. Dried mushrooms should be stored in air-tight containers in a cool dry place. Dried mushrooms can also be ground into mushroom powder which can be used for making mushroom soup. This powder being highly hygroscopic must be packed in perfectly air-tight can to prevent caking and loss of quality.

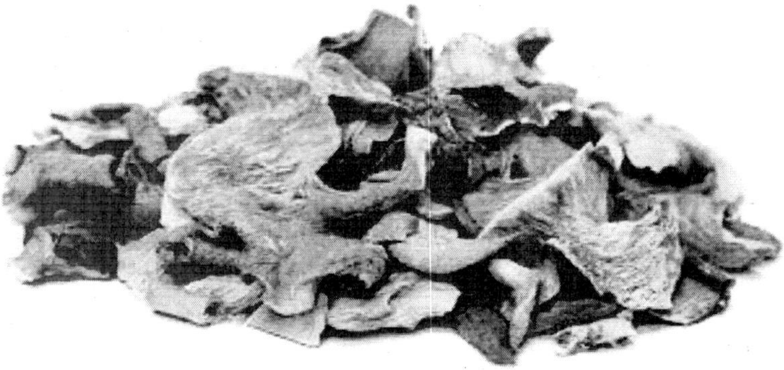

**Dried mushroom**

Mushrooms can also be dried after steam or water blanching, sulphiting and drying at 60-70°C. Dipping in the aqueous solution of chlorine, following sulphiting has been reported to give whiteness to the product. Dried mushrooms in hermetically sealed packages retain original colour and flavour for 6-7 months during storage. These are better reconstituted by inmersing in an aqueous solution of sugar and ascorbic acid.

**Freeze drying**

It is done by immersing the sliced mushrooms in a solution of 0.05% sodium metabisulphite and 2% salt for about 30 minutes. These are then blanched in boiling water for two minutes followed by cooling. The product is frozen at -22°F for one minute. The frozen mushrooms are dried to a moisture content of 3 per cent in a freeze drier and packed in cans under vacuum.

# UNIT - 13
# PREPARATION OF COIRPITH COMPOST

During the process of coir manufacturing from coconut husk, fibre dust along with baby fibers of various dimension accumulate. Every year in Tamil Nadu, about 1.5 lakh tonne of coirpith being wasted and they are heaped on roadsides causing disposal and pollution problems. Coirpith has higher C:N ratio 112 : 1 and application of fresh coirpith to field is deleterious to crop growth. Coirpith can be composted to a good compost with reduced C:N ratio of 24:1 with the help of mushroom fungus *Pleurotus sajorcaju* and *P.platypes*. However mushrooms are not produced in coirpith composting method.

**Coir waste**

**Materials**

| | | |
|---|---|---|
| Coirpith | - | 1000 kg |
| Urea | - | 5 kg |
| Oyster mushroom spawn bag | - | 5 nos. (1500 g) |

1. Spread about 100 kg coirpith uniformly in a shade place (5 x 3 m).
2. Remove the spawn from bottle and spray on the coirpith surface.
3. Spread second layer of 100 kg coirpith over first layer and sprinkle 1 kg area uniformly on the second layer.
4. Repeat this sandwiching process of one layer coirpith and mushroom spawn another layer of coirpith upto 1 m height.
5. Sprinkle water now and then to maintain 200% moisture (by touching coirpith, one should feel the wetness).
6. Allow the heap to decompose for a month.

**Coir pith manure**

## Advantages

1. Lignin content is reduced from 30% to 4.8%.
2. C:N ratio is narrowed down from 112% to 24%.
3. 'N' content is also increased from 0.26% to 1.06%.
4. Composted coir pith is rich in micro, macro and secondary nutrients.
5. Beneficial to dry land and alkali soils.
6. Improve the water holding capacity and physical characters of soils.

**Table 7 Nutrient status of coir pith**

| Nutrient | Before Decomposition | After Decomposition |
|---|---|---|
| N | 0.26 | 1.10 |
| P | 0.05 | 0.10 |
| K | 0.80 | 1.20 |
| Ca | 0.40 | 0.50 |
| Mg | 0.36 | 0.48 |
| Fe | 0.07 | 0.09 |
| Mn | 1.25 | 5.5 |
| Zn | 5.00 | 12.5 |
| Cu | 2.90 | 5.00 |
| C% | 30.00 | 24.20 |
| C:N | 112:1 | 24:1 |
| Lignin | 30.0 | 8.0 |
| Cellulose | 25 | 10.0 |
| pH | 5.4 | 5.8 |
| Colour | Pink | Brown to Black |
| Volume | 100 | 60 |

# UNIT - 14
# MUSHROOM FARMING - A PROFITABLE BUSINESS

A mushroom farming business can be a means of big profit in just a few weeks with considerably low start-up capital investment to start a business.

A person who has a little bit of idea in the science & technology of mushroom growing and has their own building for having the farm – mushroom business will be the perfect option for him to start. The cultivation of mushrooms is an art and requires both study and experience.

Here are the basic steps to follow to start a profitable mushroom farming business:

Attractive Opportunities in the Mushroom Cultivation Market

CAGR
**4.0%**

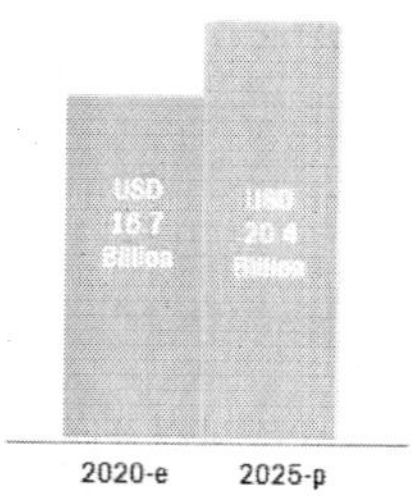


- The mushroom cultivation market is estimated to be valued at USD 16.7 billion in 2020.
- Increasing per capita consumption across globe, consumer demand for vegan, gluten-free and natural food, and food safety certification supported by frequent laboratory tests are some of the factors driving the growth in the mushroom cultivation market.

e - Estimated; p - Projected Source: Related Research Publications, Government Publications, Company Press Releases, Company Annual Reports, Company Websites, Company Publications, and MarketsandMarkets Analysis

### 1. Mushroom Farming Expertise

An individual who has worked before on a mushroom farm can start his own mushroom farming business. Otherwise, it is always better to have technical training on mushroom farming to gain expertise. You can contact Tamilnadu Agricultural University.

### 2. Write a Mushroom Farming Business Plan

Starting a small business like mushroom farming requires some specific business plan. Work out a detailed budget; write out a clear strategy and objectives for your business, what will be the variety you want to grow, and what will be your target market like domestic or export.

### 3. Choose the Type/Variety For Mushroom Farming

Different types of mushrooms have different production cost and it is important to decide on a budget depending on the amount of money available and the long term investment benefit.

Broadly, there are three types of mushrooms that are cultured. They are Button Mushroom, Oyster Mushroom, and Paddy Straw Mushroom.

A good variety to start mushroom farming with is the Oyster mushroom. Other profitable and easy to grow varieties are Milky, Paddy straw, Shiitake and White Button.

### 4. Environment For Mushroom Farming

In a mushroom farming business consider the environment for mushroom production. Different varieties require a different kind of environment. For example, the oyster mushroom has some basic environment requirements like the temperature of 15 to 20°c, the humidity of 80 to 90%, good ventilation, light, and sanitation.

## 5. Get Spawn for Mushroom Farming

You will need to have spawned to start the culture. You can produce your own spawn by using a sterile culture or you can buy ready-to-inoculate spawns form the suppliers. Producing spawns can be cheaper in the long run, because the startup cost will be high in this case.

## 6. Prepare Substrate For Mushroom Farming

Mushroom can be cultivated on a large number of agro-waste having cellulose and lignin that helps in more enzyme production of cellulose that is correlated with more yield. You can use straw of paddy, wheat and ragi, stalk and leaves of maize millets and cotton, sugarcane bagasse, sawdust, jute and cotton waste, dried grasses, used tea leaf waste, etc.

You can also use some industrial waste like paper mill sludge, coffee by-products, tobacco waste, etc. Some of the popular methods of substrate preparation are steam pasteurization, hot water treatment, fermentation of composting, and chemical sterilization.

## 7. Pack the bags/ Boxes/ Trays for mushroom farming

The bag making process normally involves composting the substrate, filling the bags with composted material, spawning and then incubation till maturity stage.

## 8. Incubation for mushrooms

Arrange the spawned bags/ boxes/ trays in a dark cropping room on raised platform concentrate to stop any threats any natural light getting into the room. Keep the growing area at a specific temperature that depends on the variety.

## 9. Fruiting in mushroom farming

While various species require different temperature regimes all require high humidity 70-80% during fruiting. Frequent spraying of water is necessary for the cropping room depending upon the environmental humidity.

## 10. Protection measures in storing mushrooms

The mushroom is suspect to attacks from flies' springtails and mites. The crop is prone to fungal disease and also can have the diseases of yellow blotch, brown spot, etc. you will need to have some specific control measure according to the attacks.

## 11. Mushroom farming harvesting & storage

The right shape for harvesting can be judged by the shape and size of the fruit body. The mushroom should be harvested before spore releases. It is advisable to pick the mushrooms at one time from a cube.

There are two types of storage involves in mushroom processing- long term and short term. Freshly harvested mushrooms can be stored at low temperatures (0-5°c) for a maximum of two weeks. Dried mushroom with 2-4% moisture, can be stored for 3-4 months in sealed pouches without any change in taste.

## 12. Mushroom farming marketing

High-quality commercial cultivation of mushrooms is a very profitable proposition as it is in good demand both in the domestic and foreign markets. You can go for local market penetration by making available your product to the retailer and vegetable shop. Also, you can go for an export option. The export market is mainly the USA, with some quantities going to the UAE, Russia, Germany, Switzerland, UK and other countries.

## Economics of mushroom cultivation

### Fixed capital

| S.No. | Description | Cost (Rs.) |
|---|---|---|
| 1 | Mushroom shed | 60,000.00 |
| 2 | Smokeless wood stove | 2,000.00 |
| 3 | Drum | 2,000.00 |
| 4 | Polythene sheet 10 x 12 ft 2 nos | 2,000.00 |
| 5 | Sprayer | 1000.00 |
| 6 | Plastic bucket 2 nos | 600.00 |
| 7 | Big knife | 200.00 |
| 8 | Sealing machine | 3,500.00 |
| 9 | Physical balance | 2,500.00 |
|  | Total | 73,800.00 |

### Working capital

| S.No. | Description | Cost (Rs.) |
|---|---|---|
| 1 | Paddy straw 2 tons @Rs.4000/ton | 8,000.00 |
| 2 | Polythene bag 3840 no @ Rs.2.50/bag | 8,640.00 |
| 3 | Spawn 1920 pkt/(200 grm pkt) @ Rs.25/pkt | 48,000.00 |
| 4 | Wood (Fuel) | 3,500.00 |
| 5 | Pesticide | 1,000.00 |
| 6 | Pocketing bag 11232 nos @ 0.50/bag | 5,616.00 |
|  | Total | **74,756.00** |
|  | Grand Total (73,800 + 74,756) | **1,48,556.00** |

### Economic benefit of mushroom

| S.No. | Description |  |
|---|---|---|
| 1 | Room size | = 25 ft x 15 ft x 8 ft |
| 2 | Capacity | = 480 bags (at a time) |
| 3 | Crop duration | = 45 days |
| 4 | Total no. of bags produces in a year | = 480 x 8 = 3840 bags |
| 5 | Production per bag | = 750 g |
| 6 | Total production in a year | = 750 x 3840 = 2880 kg |

| | | |
|---|---|---|
| 7 | Considering 2.5% production loss | = 72 kg |
| 8 | Net production | = 2880-72 = 2808 kg |
| 9 | Selling price @ Rs.160 per kg (Raw) | |
| 10 | Total selling price | = 2808 x 160 = Rs.4,49,280 |
| 11 | Total expenditure | = Rs.1,48,556/- |
| 12 | Total profit (yearly) | = (449280-148556)=Rs.300724/- |
| 13 | Cost : benefit ratio | =1:2.02 |

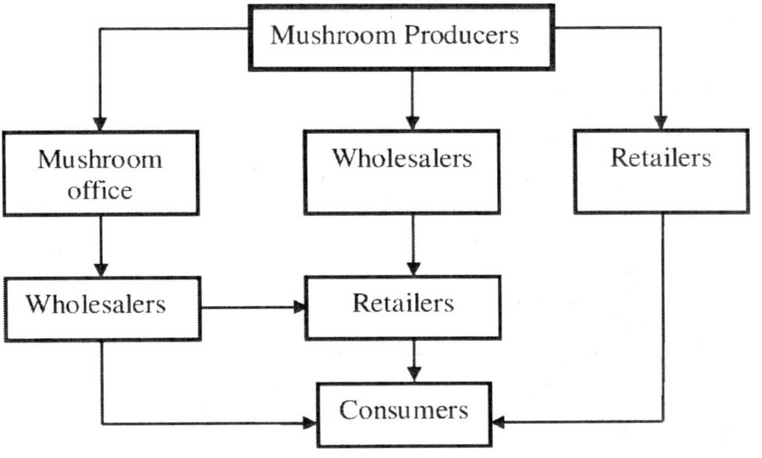


**Marketing channels of mushroom production**

**Mushroom marketing**

1. Expand the market area and strengthen the demand

a. Popularize mushrooms using Information communication technology(ICT) as delicacy with nutritive and medicinal value, on mass media like Doordarshan , radio also ads. and posters.

b. Break consumer resistance by creating awareness in new areas. Demonstration of recipes and free samples in new areas. Free recipe booklet.

2. Form cooperatives for sale.
    a. Create cold storage facility
    b. Create refrigerated transport facility
    c. Create processing facility
    d. Create distributor function for big cities.
3. Decrease the cost of production and bring down the sale price to boost the demand.
4. Good pre packs for eye appeal.
5. Train retailers about handling, storage, food value and recipes.
6. Approach supermarkets, chain vegetable stores, dairy retail counters for retail sale.
7. States should fix minimum support price.

8. Public sector marketing, processing and export organisations should come forward.
9. Assured supply throughout the year at a reasonable constant price is key to good marketing. Efforts should be made to diversify and cultivate different mushrooms throughout the

year along with cultivating some of the important mushroom during off-season under controlled condition.

10. In a limited area, say a village or a cooperative, the crops should be time-scheduled to get a daily reasonably uniform production to avoid glut on a day, this is required to meet the commensurate demand
11. Star hotels can be invited to popularise the different recipes made out of mushrooms among the customers
12. Dieticians of different nursing home or medicals can be invited and make them understand about the mushroom which provide a rich addition to the diet in the form of protein, carbohydrate, valuable salt, vitamins &minerals, amino acid and energy.

13. Contact the Cooking masters of local area or nearby cities. Canvass them to cook mushroom briyani instead of vegetable briyani in the family functions like marriage, birth day, anniverrsary, etc.
14. Contact and canvass bakerys to introduce mushroom puffs and other mushroom based bakery items.

15. Collect and contact the phone numbers of those who are printing invitations for their family function from the printing press for the sale of mushroom.
16. Contact all the platform snack stalls of nearby towns. Canvass them to introduce mushroom bonda, bajji and other mushroom based snacks.
17. Contact the samosa whole sale seller, ask them to introduce mushroom samosa.
18. Contact the chicken/mutton soup sellers ask them to introduce mushroom soup.
19. Contact the daily/weekly market in the towns and villages, put retail mushroom stalls.
20. Contact all the hotels to introduce mushroom briyani.

# UNIT - 15
# INDIAN MUSHROOM RECIPES

## 1. Mushroom soup

| | | |
|---|---|---|
| Fresh mushrooms | - | 50g |
| Onion | - | 1 no |
| Ginger | - | 10 g |
| Garlic Cloves | - | 5 nos |
| Maida flour | - | 1 teaspoon |
| Milk | - | one cup |
| Ghee | - | 1 teaspoon |
| Salt | - | Required quantity |
| Pepper | - | Required quantity |

Wash the mushroom and onion. Cut the same into pieces. Mix the mushroom pieces, onion pieces, ginger, and garlic cloves. Boil the above said mixture in 3/4$^{th}$ litre of water. Fry the above said mixture and maida flour with milk and allow it to boil for 5-10 minutes. Add salt and pepper to taste. Now the soup is ready to serve.

**Mushroom soup**

## 2. Canned mushroom soup

| | | |
|---|---|---|
| Fresh mushrooms | – | 500 g |
| Butter | – | 50 g |
| White flour (Maida) | – | 50 g |
| Salt | – | Required quantity |
| Ground spices (cardamom, red chilies, cinnamon and pepper) | – | 4 g |
| Milk | – | 1 litre |

Take any edible variety of fresh mushrooms, clean them carefully in water. Blend them well in a waring blender or a meat mincer. Pass this slurry through an aluminum or plastic sieve to remove the fibrous portion. Melt butter in a pan and fry the slurry till it is just brown. Add to it white flour, salt, spices and milk and boil the whole mass to a thick consistency of a heavy cream. The soup is ready for use.

For canning purposes fill the boiling hot soup into one lb grain cans leaving about one cm head space. Immediately seal the cans and process them at 115°C for 30 minutes cool, these cans and place them in a cool dry place. Keep the soup can in boiling water for 10 minutes before serving

## 3. Pickles

Pickles made with the mushrooms can be packed in jars. Pour over them highly spiced, scalding vinegar. Allow them to stand for at least two weeks.

| | | |
|---|---|---|
| Fresh mushrooms | - | 500 g |
| Salt | - | 28 g |
| Ginger (ground) | - | 4g |
| Onion (chopped) | - | 15 g |
| Pepper | - | 2 g |
| Nutmeg | - | 1 g |
| Vinegar | - | Required quantity |

Use mushrooms, while they are in the round or button stage. Immerse them in cold water for a few minutes and drawn them. Put them clean mushrooms in a pan with sufficient vinegar to cover and add the rest of the ingredients. Allow them for 10 minutes and pour the whole material into small glass jars taking care that all the spices are divided equally among each jar and the mushrooms are covered with hot vinegar. The jars are allowed to stand for a day when these are the sealed.

**Mushroom pickles**

**4. Mushroom cutlet**

| | | |
|---|---|---|
| Fresh mushrooms | - | 250 g |
| Potatoes | - | 100 g |
| Bellary onion | - | 100g |
| Peeled green peas | - | 50 g |
| Bengal gram flour | - | 150 g |
| Green chillies | - | 5 nos |
| Coriander leaves | - | Small quantity |
| Turmeric powder | - | Small quantity |
| Oil | - | Required quantity |

Wash and cut the mushroom into small pieces. Boil the green peas. Boil, the potatoes and peel off the skin and make it into a paste. Cut the onion, green chillies and coriander leaves into small pieces. Grind the ginger into a paste. Mix the boiled green peas, onion, green chillies, coriander leaves and potato paste. Add turmeric powder, chilli powder and salt to taste. Make the above mixture into a ball. Dip the ball in bengal gram flour paste. Fry it in oil and the cutlet is ready to serve.

**Mushroom cutlet**

### 5. Mushroom Kuruma

| | | |
|---|---|---|
| Fresh mushroom | - | 250 g |
| Bellary onion | - | 50 g |
| Tomato | - | 100 g |
| Green chillies | - | 15 g |
| Garlic | - | 1 no |
| Ginger | - | small quantity |
| Coconut grated | - | 2 table spoons |
| Aniseed | - | 1/2 teaspoon |
| Ghee | - | 1 teaspoon |
| Salt | - | Required quantity |
| Oil | - | Required quantity |
| All spices | - | Required quantity (small quantity) |

Wash the mushrooms. Cut into pieces, slice the onions, green chillies and tomato. Fry the aniseed, poppy seeds and coconut mixture. To this add garlic cloves, and ginger and make it to paste. Fry the sliced leaf mixture. Add required quantity of water and salt and boil it. Add little ghee for better results.

**Mushroom kuruma**

**6. Mushroom briyani**

| | | |
|---|---|---|
| Fresh mushrooms | - | 250 g |
| Briyani rice | - | 1 kg |
| Carrot | - | 100 g |
| Cauliflower | - | 100 g |
| Cabbage | - | 100 g |
| Bellary onion | - | 150 g |
| Green chillies | - | 25 g |
| Coconut grated | - | 2 nos |
| Fennel | - | 2 teaspoon |
| Mint, coriander and culty leaf | - | 1 bundle |

| | | |
|---|---|---|
| Turmeric powder | - | Required quantity |
| Green peas | - | 50 g |
| Ginger | - | Small pieces |
| Salt | - | Required quantity |
| Oil | - | Required quantity |

Cut mushroom and vegetables to pieces. Slice the onion, tomato and green chillies. Take coconut milk from the coconut grates. Grind the fennel, garlic, ginger, and turmeric powder together. Fry the cut and sliced ingredients and cinnamon leaf in dalda. Add the cut mint leaves, curry leaf and coriander leaves to this. After the vegetables get fried add the paste made out of garlic and ginger. Add the briyani rice after due cleaning, to the above mixture. When half boiled add coconut milk. Cook, stiring constantly in medium heat serve hot.

# REFERENCES

1. Alice, D., M. Muthusamy and I. Yesuaja. 1999. Mushroom Culture. Agricultural College and Research Institute, Madurai.
2. Harper, E., F.C. Miller and B.J. Macauley. 1992. Physical management and interpretation of an environmentally controlled composting ecosystem. **Australian Journal of Experimental Agriculture** 32,657-667.
3. Gulliver, A., F.C. Miller, B.J. Harper and B.J. Macauley. 1992. Environmentally controlled composting on commercial scale in Australia. **Mushroom Science** 13, 155-164.
4. Laborde, J.1992.Composting: Current and future techniques in France and in abroad. **Mushroom Information** 3, 4-24.
5. Laborde, J.1993. Required qualities of indoor composting M**ushroom Information** 9, 5-27.
6. Mantel, E. F.K., R.K. Agarwala and P.K. Seth. 1972. A guide to Mushroom cultivation Ministry of Agriculture and information unit, Directorate of Extention. New Delhi. Farm **Bull. 2.**
7. Marimuthu, T, A.G. Krishnamoorthy, K. Sivaprakasam and R. Jeyarajan. 1989.Oyster Mushroom Production. Tamil Nadu Agricultural University, Coimbatore.
8. Sharma, V.P., K.A. Sudheer, G. Yogesh, S. Manjit and Shwet Kamal. 2017. **Mushroom Research** 26(2): 111-120.
9. Straatsma, G., T.W. Olijnsma, J.G. Gerrits, L.J.L.D. Van Griensvan and M. Opden Camp. 1995. Inoculation of indoor phase II Compost with thermopiles. Science and Cultivation of Edible Fungi (Elliott.ed.), Balkema, Rotterda. p.283-288.